&arabs israelis

By the same authors

SAUL FRIEDLÄNDER

Pius XII and the Third Reich
Knopf, 1966

Prelude to Downfall: Hitler and the United States, 1939–1941
Knopf, 1967

Kurt Gerstein
Knopf, 1969

Réflexions sur l'avenir d'Israël
Le Seuil, 1969, 1971

L'Antisémitisme Nazi: Histoire d'une psychose collective
Le Seuil, 1971

*Histoire et Psychanalyse: Essai sur les possibilités et
les limites de la psychohistoire*
Le Seuil, 1975

MAHMOUD HUSSEIN

Les Arabes au présent
Le Seuil, 1974

Class Conflict in Egypt: 1945–1970
Monthly Review Press, 1974

&arabs &israelis

A DIALOGUE

Saul Friedländer | Mahmoud Hussein

moderated by — JEAN LACOUTURE

translated by
Paul Auster
and
Lydia Davis

HOLMES & MEIER PUBLISHERS, INC.

New York • London

First published in the United States of America 1975 by
Holmes & Meier Publishers, Inc.
101 Fifth Avenue
New York, New York 10003

Great Britain:
Holmes & Meier Publishers, Ltd.
Hillview House
1, Hallswelle Parade, Finchley Road
London, NW11 0DL

English Translation © 1975 by Holmes & Meier Publishers, Inc.

© Editions du Seuil 1974

Originally published as *Arabes & Israéliens: Un premier dialogue*
by Editions du Seuil

LIBRARY OF CONGRESS CATALOGING IN PUBLICATION DATA

Hussein, Mahmoud.
   Arabs and Israelis.
   Translation of Arabes & Israéliens in which the authors' names
appeared in reverse order.
   1. Jewish-Arab relations—1967-1973—Addresses, essays,
lectures. 2. Jewish-Arab relations—1973-   —Addresses,
essays, lectures. I. Friedländer, Saul, 1932-
joint author. II. Lacouture, Jean. III. Title.
DS119.7.H9313   327.5694'017'4927   75-9147
ISBN 0-8419-0208-9

CONTENTS

AFTERWORDS TO THE AMERICAN EDITION   *209*

Foreword

A New Beginning

Has there ever really been a "first dialogue" since the Garden of Eden? Men have always managed to arrive at some form of communication—Greeks with Trojans, Turks with Moors, Sitting Bull with Buffalo Bill, policemen with hippies. But that day, when we brought together Mahmoud Hussein and Saul Friedländer, we all believed that something strange was about to begin, and that it might be something good. Three days later, we all knew that "first" or not, this dialogue had measured up to the expectations we had had for so long.

Simonne Lacouture and I had been hoping to make this contact ever since our involvement with Giorgio La Pira in Florence. There, with the help of some friends, we had not only tried to open up lines of communication with the Algerian FLN, still underground, but also to bring together Cypriots from both sides, and to arrange a meeting between Nahum Goldmann and an Egyptian intellectual as boldly unusual as Georges Henein. Two years ago, Israeli historian Saul Friedländer, who had published his excellent works on Roosevelt, Nazism, and Pope Pius XII with us, suggested that he hold a discussion with a representative Arab intellectual who was willing at last to break the silence of a quarter of a century, and that a book be formed from this discussion. Until October of 1973 that hope had come to nothing. No true Israeli, citizen of a state founded on Zionism and basically dedicated to its ideological principles and political disciplines, was acceptable to any of the possible Arab candidates. And wasn't the victorious enemy less powerful if the Arabs refused to speak to him? By keeping silent, by refusing to look at him, they denied his existence. And if he really did exist, they could not talk to him without being humiliated, without making him seem all the more imposing, without implicitly acknowledging the "rightness" of his position. Silence was not victory, nor equality, but it was the denial of the enemy's victory, and the only form of equality possible.

Then, at the height of the October 1973 war, a letter from Mahmoud Hussein published in *Le Nouvel Observateur* declared that the time for Arab silence was past, just as the time was past when the Arabs had seemed unable to defend themselves. Of course there are many objections to drawing a connection between the "dignity" of a people and its prowess in war. But there may be fewer objections in the case of the Jewish people, whose hope and pride were restored by the amazing battle waged by Anilewicz and his comrades in the Warsaw ghetto at a time when the Jews were being scattered and decimated.

Mahmoud Hussein's letter released the Arab world from its vow of silence toward Israel. The letter did not speak of peace. It simply spoke of the others, like the book by the same author—*Les Arabes au présent* [The Arabs Today]—which appeared shortly afterwards. And that was enough to offer a basis for hope, perhaps a more effective basis than the negotiations, which from Km 101 to the offices of the State Department had resulted only in pathetic little agreements. It is obviously a good thing that the wounds are being bandaged up and the troops are being withdrawn from several occupied areas. But these technical gestures will not become meaningful until the imaginations and feelings of a great many people give them the kind of support which only a few people have been giving them up to now.

Are Saul Friedländer and Mahmoud Hussein among those few? Saul Friedländer, who was born in Czechoslovakia six years before

Munich and whose parents were killed at Auschwitz, lived in France until the age of sixteen and adopted Israel as his country the same year it was proclaimed a Jewish state. He is a distinguished historian, a professor at the Hebrew University of Jerusalem and the Graduate Institute of International Studies in Geneva, and he belongs to the intellectual establishment of Israel. He was apparently in close touch with government circles for a long time (even though his book *Réflexions sur l'avenir d'Israël* [Reflections on the Future of Israel] brilliantly develops viewpoints that are quite different from those held by Mrs. Meir), but he has gradually approached what could be called the liberal current of thought of Jerusalem's intelligentsia, which though it maintains its link with the leading parties, is in favor of more active attempts to achieve a form of peace that combines justice with security. Liberal in the Anglo-Saxon tradition, nonreligious, nurtured as much on German science as on French culture, haunted by the atrocities of the Third Reich, to which he has devoted several penetrating books, working now on a book about psychohistory, estranged from Marxism without ignoring what it has contributed, and deeply committed to Zionism, Saul Friedländer is a highly representative spokesman for Israel's politico-intellectual class, less because he fits into its sociological context than because he dynamically conveys its fruitful disquiet.

It is not easy to introduce Mahmoud Hussein, if only because he is more than one man. The pseudonym is shared by two Egyptians who have each recently turned thirty and who have divided their lives among militant activism, prison, and exile. Five years of penal servitude in the Egyptian desert under Nasser have not affected their revolutionary convictions. They have been Communists since their adolescence, and are held to be Maoists by some of their friends and many of the readers of *Class Conflict in Egypt,* a book which presented an impressive leftist critique of Nasserism and made its authors known to Europeans and young Arabs four years ago. They remain dedicated to Marxism as a method and as a view of history. The uncertain progress of the Arab world toward unification has not discouraged them in their hope that such a unification will be the basis for a general movement against the present ruling classes of the Middle East,

ix

whether feudal or bourgeois. The movement would be against the ruling classes, but who would join in the movement? For Mahmoud Hussein, that is the subject of this book...

Can the author of *Les Arabes au présent* be considered just as representative of Arab-Moslem culture as Saul Friedländer is of the Judeo-Israeli community? Mahmoud Hussein's voice is the voice of the avant-garde, informed by militancy and Marxism, and reflecting long acquaintance with political circles in the West. And anyone who has had experience in the Arab world will certainly hear, too, an echo of the popular voice, the noisy outbursts typical of the style of reasoning—usually less coherent and less knowledgeable than Mahmoud Hussein's—which gives life to the discussions heard by the people of Cairo and Damascus. His historical situation places Mahmoud Hussein for the time being at the edge of Arab politics with all its many fluctuations—but his sensibility is profoundly identified with the sensibility of young Arabs everywhere, from Casablanca to the Gulf of Oman. And he is also representative of them in being courageous enough to break the silence at last.

These were the men who confronted one another in Paris and joined in discussion from the 25th to the 27th of July 1974. We had agreed to come together around a tape recorder for at least three days, basing our discussion on a rough plan worked out by Hussein and Friedländer. The fact that I was a friend of each of the three made me the choice for moderator. I thought I would have to intervene often, at first to break the ice, then to cool off the atmosphere, or even to stop fights. It should be clear from the text—only its form has been touched up, and touched up as little as possible in order to preserve the natural and spontaneous quality of the debate—that instead my role moved back and forth between gadfly and master of ceremonies. Which pleases me, since I gauge the richness of a dialogue by how little the third person says.

It might seem surprising that Mahmoud Hussein sometimes says "we" and sometimes "I." We agreed not to establish any strict rule about this, or about the number of times anyone spoke, the amount said in support of any one point, or the length of the debate as a whole. When the end of the third day came, however, it seemed to all of us that what needed to be said had been said. We were not there to make peace, or to lay down plans for peace, or even to make an appeal to the world or write a good book. More than anything else we were there to show that a lively exchange of views is more fertile than a fight to the death.

As I opened the debate I had an uneasy thought. The debate is taking place, I said to myself, and that is wonderful. But how will it end? How can it come to an end without one of them wanting to make one last remark in reply to the other? And when at the end of the third afternoon Mahmoud Hussein had finished the last thing he had to say, it was not without a certain apprehension that I turned toward Saul Friedländer. What he said or did not say after fifty years of fighting, twenty-five years of war and silence, three days of debating, proved to us all that our meeting had not been in vain. But how can I convey the significance of that silence to someone who has not yet read this book?

Read it.

Jean Lacouture

&arabs
israelis

I

First Day: The Past

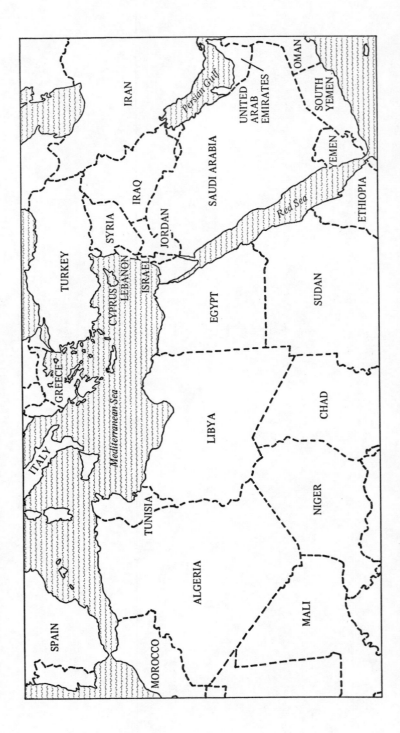

JEAN LACOUTURE: Since I don't want to hold up this discussion, which we've been waiting for so eagerly, I will start it off by simply asking you both two banal questions: Why did we have to wait so long for this discussion? And why has it become possible to hold it now, in July of 1974?

SAUL FRIEDLÄNDER: It is not without some emotion that I enter into this dialogue which we Israelis have been anticipating for such a long time, not only since the creation of the State of Israel, but since the beginning of Zionism, since the beginning of the organized return of the Jews to Palestine. The Arabs have always refused to hold this dialogue and it is only in the last few months, for the first time, that there has been a noticeable change in their attitude.

I hope all the various contacts that have been made recently are not just another episode, but evidence of a fundamental change in the feelings of the Arab world, in other words, the first step toward the possible resolution of a conflict that has set us against one another for more than half a century.

In fact we, the Israelis, think that without dialogue, without direct, human contact between the antagonists, true peace can hardly even be imagined. This is not a territorial dispute that other people can settle for us but a confrontation on a deep psychological

3

level, where the accumulation of mistrust and the most negative stereotypes on both sides play a predominant role. In these circumstances dialogue, direct contact, becomes an essential element in the resolution of the conflict.

This makes me think of the special issue of *Les Temps Modernes* devoted to the Arab-Israeli conflict that came out just before the Six Day War. As you remember, there were two sections in it, one Israeli and one Arab. In his introduction, Claude Lanzmann spoke of "inert coexistence." I think it was even less than that. Anyway, I'm sure you remember the title of the last article in the Arab section: "Why Are We Saying 'No' To Dialogue?"

That was seven years ago, and it had been the same for fifty years. But here we are now, after all, gathered together, and the question we are opening the debate with is "Why Are We Saying 'Yes' To Dialogue?" What a difference.

No one has any illusions about how difficult the task is that we have embarked on. Real peace will not be achieved tomorrow or the day after. But I'm going to say something that might seem paradoxical. Even if the fighting has to start up again—and of course we're all hoping that it won't have to—this dialogue and the other contacts that have taken place in the past few months could still bring about a change in the very nature of the conflict. If more and more of these initiatives take place, they might represent the beginning of an irreversible movement toward reestablishing good relations. For me, as an Israeli, this is an important day.

MAHMOUD HUSSEIN: It is really up to the Arabs to explain why, after having refused for so long to enter into a dialogue, they have agreed to it now.

The anwer is not simple. It requires a return to the past—something we would have preferred to avoid, since we are trying to focus on the present and examine the future. So this detour into the past should be brief. Its purpose is to take a fresh look at the future; it only interests us insofar as it affects the future.

I should make one thing clear right away before going any further. Though I will sometimes be forced to talk about Arabs in general, we should keep in mind the fact that the Arab world is made up of numerous states, which are themselves split up into various social classes. Among these different nations and social forces there is no one attitude toward the Arab-Israeli conflict. Therefore, when I use the undifferentiated term "Arab," I will be referring to a broad current of opinion, diffuse and imprecise, a sum total of disparate forces which in my opinion expresses a general tendency, even if there is no recognized spokesman for that tendency and even if it isn't something immediately obvious to those on the outside. But I will try to be specific as often as possible, especially when I'm dealing with particular problems.

A dialogue is part of a total process of changing things. It has no meaning except as it takes part in this process and helps it to move forward in a useful way. I think we would like to know why the situation as it is now allows for a useful dialogue, and how far it will allow us to go.

The attitude of the Arabs in the last half century toward the Jewish national home and then the State of Israel has not been uniform or consistent. It has varied from region to region. The Palestinians, of course, were the first to be confronted by Zionist colonization. During the same period the problem was recognized by the rest of the Machrek*—which included what are now Syria, Jordan, Lebanon, Israel, and Iraq. But as far as the other Arab nations, including Egypt, were concerned, the Zionist settlement in Palestine was something distant, something nebulous, not a constant preoccupation. Beyond the Machrek, the problems posed by the State of Israel after its founding at the end of the 1948-1949 war were somehow the exclusive concern of Arab political leaders. Of course the people tended to side with the Palestinians on specific issues, but for them it was only of secondary importance.

The example of Egypt is striking. From 1945 to 1947 a very widespread popular movement arose against the British military occupation. When the Palestinian war began in 1948, there was a temporary halt in the fighting against Britain, and public opinion was roused behind the Arab volunteers and soldiers, against the army of a state which was quite naturally regarded as a dangerous

*As opposed to the Maghreb, which is the Western part of the Arab world. The Machrek is roughly equivalent to what is commonly called the Levant. It does not include Egypt.

foreign presence. But once the war was over everyone's attention was focused again, even more intensely, on Egypt's own targets: the English army on the canal, the corrupt monarchy, and the outmoded party system. The Arab defeat in Palestine became one more argument in favor of the people's fight against the monarchy and the British presence, which were regarded as responsible for the humiliation that had been suffered.

Even when Nasser began to bring up the question of Israel several years after coming to power, he always held back from taking action. Until 1967 the Egyptian people put up with the idea that Nasser would make a move to repair the injustice done to the Palestinians only when he felt the time was ripe. And that seemed like the best thing to do. The idea people had formed of Israel was in general quite simple: Israel was a pawn of imperialism and had no reason for existing other than to serve one of the great powers in its anti-Arab plans. It was nothing but a small island of foreign territory, an extension of the West that had been implanted with violence and trickery in the heart of the Arab world, an artificial creation without the least authenticity which fed off the umbilical cord tying it to Europe and the United States.

Nasser was trying to rid the Arab world of foreign domination, and in the end he would take care of this problem. Very few people thought about it any more than that, and no one asked himself what "taking care of Israel" really meant.

June 1967 ended this period of innocence. The Arabs awoke to the fact that Israel was a very substantial reality, and one which seemed all the more formidable because it had seemed so negligible before; they saw that the danger Israel represented concerned not only the Palestinians but all the countries that bordered on Israel; and that in the long run Israel was a threat to all the other Arab countries as well. This was more than a decade after Nasser had asked the Egyptian people to make large material sacrifices to allow him to organize an army powerful enough to guard against all outside dangers, including an American-directed attack by Israel.

And then in June 1967, in the space of several days, that army, around which a whole mythology had grown up, was singlehandedly swept away along with the armies of Syria and Jordan by the Israeli army—financed and equipped by the West, it is true, but fighting alone. From that time on there was no way any

Egyptian, no matter how apolitical he was, could ignore the importance of Israel. Part of Egypt was occupied; the Suez Canal, the symbol of the nation's dignity which had been taken back from the British army several years earlier, became the symbol of another national humiliation. Every Egyptian family had a father, a son, or a friend who had died or been wounded in the Sinai. From then on the problem of Israel became a domestic problem for Egypt.

JEAN LACOUTURE: Didn't the war of 1956 enlighten the Arab people about the ability of their leaders to deal with the Palestinian question? Did they see any real difference between the defeat of 1967 and the inability of the Arabs to join forces against the tripartite operation called Suez?

MAHMOUD HUSSEIN: The 1956 aggression was not considered a defeat by the Egyptian people, still less a defeat inflicted by the Israeli army. The attack was launched by Israel, yes. But the Egyptian people believed that the ones who were truly responsible, the ones who organized the aggression, were England and France. We should remember that what was at stake in this war was the Suez Canal. Given that, Israel was only playing a role which was already familiar. It was a tool of the imperialist armies and nothing more. Besides, Nasser had ordered the Egyptian army to leave the Sinai and protect the canal, and operations in the Sinai took place away from inhabited areas, whereas the English and French pilots and paratroopers were acting within sight of the inhabitants of the cities in the canal and delta areas. The popular resistance was organized against them rather than the Israeli army, which was far away, still intangible and insignificant.

Also, the Egyptian people felt that in 1956 the Egyptian army had not had time to develop, to be modernized and trained. It had been equipped with modern weapons for the first time only a year before. A military defeat under those conditions, and by the joint armies of England, France and Israel, was not dishonorable.

By 1967, that was no longer the case. The Egyptian army had no excuse; and this time Israel held center stage. From then on it cast a distinct shadow over the future. The time had come to face it squarely and try to understand what it was made up of.

To differing degrees Egypt's feelings were shared by the other Arab countries. As we have said, the Machrek did not need the Six Day War to make it deeply aware of the presence of Israel. Syria, in particular, had continuously felt that the birth of that state and the dispersal of the Palestinians was like an amputation. Syria is actually the cultural hub of the part of the Ottoman Empire that used to be called Greater Syria, which also included Palestine and Lebanon; the Arabs had expected to see it evolve into a unified and sovereign state after the First World War. The division of the area into small entities, irrationally carved out according to the whims of England and France, and the implanting of a non-Arab embryo state in Palestine were never accepted by the people. Revolutions broke out and popular movements were organized against this imperialist maneuver which placed the Arab people in a ridiculously weak and divided position and trampled indiscriminately over their dream of unification and rebirth.

So in that area, and particularly among the Palestinians—I won't talk about them at length now, but some time later, during the third day—the existence of the *Yishuv** was experienced as a collective weakness. There, in contrast to Egypt, the attitude the different political forces adopted toward the Jewish homeland played an important role. The people felt it was an integral part of the larger fight for dignity and independence.

But I should point out that though the conflict with Israel was certainly regarded as a political issue, politics in the Machrek were still strongly imbued with the traditionalist point of view in affairs of state; politics and religion could not be completely dissociated. Modern states had not been established here until after World War I. The social fabric was in the process of emerging from the despotic structures of the past; the dominant ideology mingled the spiritual and the temporal. The presence of Israel, therefore, implied that not only a part of the Arab patrimony, but also parts of the territory of Islam had been stolen. For a Moslem there was no greater shame than for that to happen. The feeling born of this was,

---

*A Hebrew term designating the Jewish community that settled in Palestine (Eretz Yisrael) before the founding of the State of Israel.

quite naturally, the desire to wipe out the insult and restore things to their proper places.

As for the Maghreb, 1967 was what really involved it in the political confrontation between the Arabs and Israel. Until then a sense of solidarity that was mainly religious and sentimental moved people to care only in a vague sort of way about the fate of Palestine. After the June war, young people who were beginning to think about the problems of political independence, who were looking for ideals of radical freedom and were roused by the call for Arab unity, suddenly saw a challenge facing them that was far greater than they had suspected before. Ever since the end of the Algerian war they had believed that the time was past when there could be foreign powers in the Arab world. And then in six days that question was raised again, with fresh urgency. On top of the humiliation shared by everyone there was the feeling that the Israeli threat was perhaps not restricted to the Middle East...

JEAN LACOUTURE: When people answer you by saying that at that time the question of Palestine served mainly as a diversion for the Arab leaders, who had little concern for looking after their own social and economic problems or were unable to do so, do you think they're mocking you, or is what they say partially true?

MAHMOUD HUSSEIN: That aspect of the situation certainly can't be dismissed. The governments of many Arab countries have often used—and continue to use—the question of Palestine as a focus for strong feelings when they want to distract the people's attention from serious domestic problems. But this has been emphasized too much in the West; it is important to see that this is only one aspect of their policy.

The problem of Israel can't be reduced to that kind of maneuvering; it is not an unreal problem, entirely fabricated by politicians in trouble. They would not be able to reach the public if strong feelings did not already exist, more profound and more direct in some places than in others. These feelings arise from the plain fact that a foreign body was inserted into the Arab world without the consent of its peoples and against the will of the ones most intimately involved. Moreover, it was a body closely tied to the imperialist presence in the area, at a moment when that presence was being fought by the Arab national movement.

That is why use of this problem by the leaders of different Arab countries was not, even from their point of view, purely Machiavellian.

The formation of the State of Israel and its integration into the network of the Western presence in the Middle East represented a challenge to the Arab governments, and soon became a threat. Take the example of Nasser. In the beginning he was not against some form of accord with Israel. This possibility of an agreement even led Foster Dulles in the years between 1952 and 1954 to think he could persuade Egypt to join Israel in an anti-Soviet military alliance. But little by little, during this same period, Nasser discovered that a profound incompatibility existed between his plans for the future and those of the Israeli leaders.

His dream was of accelerated industrialization, which would provide the solution to all of Egypt's structural problems: its thwarted development, the resulting massive unemployment, its fundamental dependence on foreign markets, and the extremely low standard of living of its people. And it went without saying that Egypt's new burst of progress, generated by modern heavy industry, couldn't have a solid and profitable basis unless the Arab world gradually broke off the channels of exchange that tied it to the West, opened its markets to Egypt, and centered its economic reorganization there. But Israel had similar ideas.

The Zionist leaders then in power, headed by Moshe Sharett, envisaged the possibility of a *modus vivendi* with the Arabs under American protection and expected, like Egypt, to see the doors of the Arab Middle East open to them. As they saw it, they would use the economy to integrate themselves into the Middle East, which means they would set up a system of exchanges in which Israel would furnish the capital, the skill, and the manufactured products, while the Arab states, whose economic level was so much lower, would furnish raw materials, agricultural products, and possibly labor. In short, the same thing would happen that is happening now on the West Bank.

In time, this reduced Nasser's plans to nothing—since a peaceful contest between Egypt and Israel for economic leadership in the Arab world would be lost by Egypt before it was begun. Israel could bring to bear against Egypt all the cultural and technological assets of the West and could channel enormous amounts of European and American capital into the Middle East through Israeli subsidiaries. In a certain way it was a consolidation of the Western presence in the heart of the Arab world—and involved not only the ruin of Nasser's cherished hopes for easing the crisis with which Egypt was struggling but at the same time was an intolerable challenge to the Palestinians, who had just been forced to leave their homeland, and an insult to the whole of the Machrek, for whom Israel was nothing but an intruder. On every level it was unthinkable to the Arabs.

Gradually Nasser came to understand that the economic aid he had hoped for from the Americans would not help him to bring about true progress in Egyptian industry and that aid would only come in driblets as he adapted his policies to the American anti-Communist tactics in the Middle East. The brutal withdrawal of America's offer to finance the Aswan Dam finally opened his eyes to this situation. In the same way, Israel's military provocations after the return of Ben-Gurion to the head of the Israeli government at the beginning of 1955 showed Nasser that the pursuit of his plan to develop his nation was causing a progressive hardening in his adversary's position. The participation of the Israeli army in the French and English aggression against Egypt in October 1956 proved unequivocally that the Israelis were prepared to do anything to prevent the birth of an autonomous Arab power.

If Israel had reacted to the nationalization of the Suez Canal by invading the Sinai Desert, what would it do when Nasser began to industrialize the country, transform his army, unify the Arab national movement?

Israel was compelled by the logic of its original political choices to oppose the Arab national movement by seeking help from the powers that wanted to maintain their domination over the area. In this context, the nationalist Arab leaders could present themselves, in confronting Israel, as representatives of the best interests of their people, and so salvage their hope for independence.

JEAN LACOUTURE: During this period did the left wing militants in Egypt that you're involved with think of making contact with the progressive forces in Israel? Was the "Arab refusal," to use Rodinson's formula, true of everyone?

MAHMOUD HUSSEIN: The question of contact between Arabs and Israelis could hardly be thought of in the Machrek, not in the situation we have been describing. In Egypt, it simply didn't come up at all. We weren't thinking about this problem on the level of a popular struggle. The Egyptian Left felt that its task was first and foremost to organize the masses in defense of their social and economic interests.

SAUL FRIEDLÄNDER: Your account of the Arab attitude has certain problematic points. Was the difference between the period before and the period after 1967 really as clear-cut as you describe it, at least in the minds of the Egyptians? Even if it was, what you say about 1967 as a turning point would logically lead to a new awareness on the part of the Arabs, and from then on their objective would not be dialogue at all but the elimination of Israel. I hope you'll explain to us how one proceeds from that position to the acceptance of Israel and the possibility of dialogue.

But I have one question about the Egyptian Left. You say: "For the Left, before 1967, the problem of Israel hardly existed." Didn't its members realize that a large part of the budget was devoted to military expenditure and as a result was not available for social reform? I can't believe that the Egyptian Left did not know that an essential part of the country's resources, which were relatively slim, was being channelled into preparation for war. So why didn't it set about trying to end the conflict in one way or another? There is a certain incoherence in the Left's attitude as you describe it.

MAHMOUD HUSSEIN: During this period one question was posed in the following simplified way: Who is the main enemy of the Egyptian people, and of the Arab peoples in general? And the answer was: The United States, which had taken the lead in world imperialism.

Within the framework of this analysis, Nasser's regime

represented a bourgeois nationalist force, more or less progressive depending on one's point of view, but whose plans did not tie in with the system of world domination which the United States wanted to establish in opposition to the Soviet bloc. And against this regime the United States had two essential advantages at its disposal: Israel, and the feudal and conservative forces of the Arab world, especially the Saudi Arabian government.

The Egyptian Left anticipated numerous attempts by this coalition of anti-nationalist forces to sabotage or crush the movement for Arab rebirth that was forming around Nasser—and it believed, particularly after the aggression of October 1956, that a powerful regular army was absolutely necessary for the defense of Egypt.

This army was not specifically preparing to destroy Israel. It had been conceived as a defensive force to guard Egypt—and the rest of the Arab world, if it possibly could—from the various dangers which threatened them. Israel was certainly one of the enemies, but not the main one. Until June of 1967, as I have said, it was regarded as no more than an auxiliary force.

SAUL FRIEDLÄNDER: Let me return to the distinction you made between Israel's lack of importance for the Egyptians before 1967 and its central importance for the Machrek—for the Syrians and Iraqis in particular. For a time Egypt and Syria were united and therefore influenced each other on all levels; the same radio stations were listened to in both places, there were constant contacts between the Egyptian and the Syrian intellectual elites, and so forth. Is the distinction you're trying to maintain really conceivable? And do the spatial and temporal divisions you establish really hold up? Wouldn't you say that even before 1967 Israel was already more than a secondary problem, even for the Egyptians, and that even they believed the Jewish state had to disappear eventually?

MAHMOUD HUSSEIN: In a dialogue like this, the tendency is naturally to simplify things. Not only was there no watertight division between Egypt's view of politics and the Machrek's, but since Nasser first came to power both regions have moved closer and closer to agreement on this question. But there is still a difference in sensibilities that arises from the histories of the two regions and is one of the political factors in the present situation.

Beyond the very strong historical and cultural ties that unite all the Arab peoples, there are important differences among them. Some go back to the time before Islam; others can be explained by what is going on right now. Unlike the Machrek, for example, Egypt was torn from the Ottoman Empire by the English in the last quarter of the nineteenth century, and the national movement developed in opposition to British colonization within a state that had been strongly centralized for thousands of years, which means that it had considerably more autonomy than the Arab world that surrounded it, until the Second World War.

The Machrek, on the other hand, was closely tied to the declining Turkish Empire until the First World War. A powerful sense of unity developed between regions which were no more than administrative entities dependent on Constantinople, without any structure of their own as states. These regions conceived of their independence as coming about within the framework of a great realm which would bring back to life the Arab grandeur of the past. That is why the carving up of that region after 1918 was felt so deeply and why it has influenced the course of political events ever since. Between the two world wars the Machrek was traumatized by being divided up in that way and by the implantation of Zionism that accompanied it.

So there are really two parallel histories, Egypt's and Syria's, with their different circumstances and different goals. And because of this, there are two sets of preoccupations, two sorts of feelings toward Israel. This difference was painfully evident to the people of the Machrek after the Second World War, when they realized the Egyptians did not see things the same way they did.

In 1958 Syria wanted to unite with Egypt in the hope that Egypt, with its political weight, its military strength, its cultural brilliance, would make up for the weakness of the Machrek states and the discord among them and would resume the struggle to bring about the great dream of Arab unity.

SAUL FRIEDLÄNDER: If I return to the same question once again, it is because everything should be as clear as possible from the very beginning of this debate, particularly when we are starting off with essential matters. You describe differences among the attitudes of various Arab groups toward Israel, and you establish geographical distinctions and distinctions across time. But at the beginning of your remarks you mentioned the existence of a general Arab feeling. What we ought to find out is whether it isn't true that for a long time Israel has had a very definite place in that general Arab feeling. You must be aware that most Israelis think the majority of Arabs, whether of the Machrek or the Maghreb, want the Jewish state to disappear. Perhaps the Machrek expects this to happen in the near future while the Maghreb takes things as they are with more patience, but in the end the wish is the same.

The basis of this debate, you see, is the acceptance of the existence of the State of Israel by the Arabs. Consequently, it is perfectly logical that even if I become insistent, I should try to make you say whether the difference between the Egyptians and the Syrians is a fundamental difference of attitude or simply a matter of subtle nuances.

MAHMOUD HUSSEIN: I know that from Israel's point of view the problem can be reduced to a single question. But in order to understand the Arab world you have settled in, you must realize that it is made up of different regions, different socio-cultural structures, different areas of sensitivity—and that these differences go back very far into the past, to a period of time well before the creation of the State of Israel.

As far as Israel is concerned, you could say that until 1967 there was no general Arab feeling about it. Until 1967 the difference between the feelings of the Egyptians and the people of the Machrek resulted from two factors. First of all, they did not see Israel within the same ideological framework. In Egypt the problem was posed in a more political way than in the Machrek. Then again, Egypt did not feel as directly involved in the conflict with Israel as the Machrek did.

Having said this, I should emphasize that one feeling, at least, was shared by the two regions. In neither of them—contrary to what is so firmly believed in the West—did the people have any desire to exterminate the Jews. Even in the Machrek, they only wanted to right the wrong that had been done to them, to wipe out the humiliation; they did not want to gratify a feeling of hatred. It is true that the specific way this reparation would be carried out was left up to their governments to decide, which is why demagogues like Amin el-Husseini* and Shukairy** were able to speak of throwing the Jews into the sea, and why they seemed to be interpreting a popular feeling when in fact they were distorting the most legitimate part of that feeling. No one was thinking about what status the Jews would have in Palestine once it was restored to the Arabs, simply because they were concentrating on recovering it first. But as we turn to the future, the important thing to remember is that a feeling of hatred for the Jewish people never grew in the hearts of the Arabs; for the Arabs, it was the Jewish state in the abstract that had come into their world as a ravaging intruder.

---

*Hajj Amin el-Husseini (al-Husayni), the "Great Mufti" of Jerusalem, a prominent Palestinian and the implacable foe of the English mandate and Zionism. During the Second World War he fled to Berlin and allied himself to the Third Reich.

**Ahmad Shukairy, a successor to the Mufti within the Palestinian movement. For years a civil servant in Saudi Arabia, he achieved notoriety in 1967 by swearing to the Jews of Israel that they would be "thrown into the sea."

The Six Day War: A Historic Dividing Line

JEAN LACOUTURE: Now that the different attitudes towards Israel have been outlined, let us pass on to the ways in which the so-called Six Day War shattered these attitudes; how Israel's lightning victory changed not only the balance of forces in the area but also the psychological, mental, and emotional relations there; and how those days in June 1967 became a sort of frontier, a historic dividing line...

MAHMOUD HUSSEIN: In June 1967 all the people who had fought Israel were brutally forced to realize that Israel existed, that it was powerful, that it was even more powerful than all the states surrounding it. From then on people felt they had to see this country as it really was. In Egypt, Israel became more and more of a daily concern; in the Machrek, it became more and more of a political problem.

And in the Machrek and Egypt alike, a new tendency appeared—a tendency for the problem of Israel to come down to the level of the people. Until then the political leaders had handled it as they thought best, but from that point on it concerned the private citizen very directly, and he began to ask questions about it. The description he had been given of the relative strength of Arab and Israeli forces had been destroyed by what had happened. He felt this very deeply, and now he wanted to see the situation

17

clearly, understand it better, face the future with full knowledge of the facts.

It is important to point out that the new generation of Palestinians actively opposed to the presence of Israel played an essential part in this awakening. It was they who made the greatest efforts to take a clear look at the emotional and semireligious feelings the people of the Machrek had toward the problem of Israel. They helped make this issue common ground between the Machrek and Egypt, where the people were not yet preoccupied with Israel. These efforts were not made by any one resistance organization but rather came about because of a general attempt to grasp the situation in revolutionary terms, and they allowed a real leap forward in Arab consciousness to take place during the years immediately following the defeat of 1967.

Very much respected for having dared to face the enemy when regular Arab armies would not, the Palestinians were the ones mainly responsible for spreading a number of new ideas which, though they did not generate a concrete and coherent analysis of the situation, did prepare the ground for a realistic appreciation of the Israeli problem. They led the most thoughtful sections of the people to distinguish between Israel—an exploitative colonial structure—and the Jews as individuals.

As they saw it, it was necessary to fight the Jews not because they were Jewish, and not because they wanted to live in Palestine, but because they had bound up their future with the imperialist domination of the area and were, in fact, the foot soldiers of an undertaking which threatened to annihilate Palestine as an entity.

At that time, these Palestinians attempted to arrive at a solution which would be acceptable to the Jews who could dissociate themselves from that undertaking. They tried to outline a workable plan for coexistence in which everyone who wished to, no matter what his religion, could live in Palestine without imposing on anyone else, free from the antagonisms that the Zionist movement had created. The plan they finally arrived at, as we know, was to form a democratic and secular state within which Jewish and Arab communities could live on an equal footing.

JEAN LACOUTURE: It would be helpful at this point if you could explain in a few words what that slogan meant, what was involved in the plan that al-Fatah worked out, apparently in cooperation with all the leftist forces of the Arab world.

MAHMOUD HUSSEIN: I should point out that though the organizations of the resistance officially announced their resolution to form a "democratic state," this was interpreted in many different ways. Some people saw it as propaganda, others as no more than a makeshift solution. But the newest members of the resistance saw it as the product of a fresh and progressive attitude toward things: it called for a revolutionary transformation of the way people throughout the region were thinking and gave the Jews a place in Palestine as a distinct community for the first time.

As things were then, this new thinking was an exceptionally important step. Though it did not come close to resolving the problem of how to integrate the Jewish community into the region, at least it tried to explore the conditions which would make Jewish settlement there successful. It is important for the West and even more for Israel to realize how innovative, even subversive, this new leap in Arab political awareness was. From here the resistance went on to look into the dual nature of the Zionist movement and began to distinguish between the persecuted Jews of Eastern and Central Europe, who were coming to Palestine to escape the pogroms or the gas chambers with the hope of establishing a community of equals, and the people responsible for the Zionist movement, who knew perfectly well that they could not carry out their plans except by involving themselves in the strategies of one or other of the colonial powers who were dominating the region.

From the point of view of the Arab revolutionaries, therefore, the war against Israel should have opened the eyes of the Jewish masses to the role they were playing, even if inadvertently, in the region and should have led them to dissociate themselves from the Zionist institution which was responsible for it.

After this the idea of a dialogue between Arabs and Israelis became possible, since theoretically this dialogue would now have a purpose: to unite the Arabs and the Israelis against all forms of imperialist domination in the Middle East. But this dialogue did not take place, because the fact that the Arabs now took Israel seriously was not the only consequence of the June 1967 war. It had also convinced the Israelis that they were so well protected by their new frontiers and by the strength of their armies that the Arabs would finally have to admit their own weakness and accept not only the existence of Israel but also its hegemony.

This being the case, few Israelis were capable of questioning the colonial basis of their state and discovering common ground with the progressive or revolutionary Arabs. A few Israelis, perhaps a few hundred, were able to do this, and their courage must be praised, but they did not represent the underlying feelings of the people. There were some contacts, some conversations at that level, but they all took place at one remove from what was really important.

On the whole, the Israelis were no longer simply seeking recognition from the Arabs, as they had been in the first years that followed the creation of the state. Now they wanted to impose themselves as the small "great power" of the region. The Israeli army had not only moved into new territory in Egypt, Syria, and Palestine, but was pushing even farther beyond, sending planes over Cairo and Damascus, commandos into Beirut, threatening Iraq, Saudi Arabia and Libya—in short, harassing the Arabs on all sides.

From this position of superiority, which they believed to be impregnable, the Israeli leaders rejected the Arab offers of compromise advanced first by Nasser and then by Sadat—which were dependent on Israeli withdrawal from occupied territories. They were particularly vehement in their rejection of the Rogers Plan, which tended in the same direction. Since the June war, they had gained the freedom to make moves independently of the United States and now, though they did not go so far as to question America's strategic interests in the area, they were able to adapt their policies to those strategies as they thought best, both because of their strong position locally and because of the problems the United States was then facing in other parts of the world. And they used this freedom of movement to show even more intransigence in the face of Arab aspirations than their American protector had.

Arabs everywhere, this time, reacted with a sense of crushing humiliation. They saw that even their combined strength was not equal to the power of this tiny state, which until 1967 they had believed to be negligible. The fact that during a certain period they had been weaker than England or France seemed quite understandable to the Arabs, but it was intolerable for them to see themselves as weaker than Israel just when they thought they were at last free of the powers that had dominated them in the past. Israel became the symbol of everything that had ever humiliated them.

However, from the very beginning the problem of independence for the Arab peoples had been identified with their search for a common identity and with the reaffirmation of their dignity. Here we enter the realm of emotions, of psychology. We are touching on cultural factors which people sometimes tend to make light of in the name of scientific rigor but which are essential for an understanding of the political facts. Demanding dignity is a way of demanding the right to self-determination for a nation that has been colonized not only on a military or economic level but also on a cultural level. In order to begin relying on itself alone, it must first establish its own identity in relation to the rest of the world.

The Arabs express this through certain kinds of feelings, reactions, appropriate references to history; it is much less easily translated into concrete resolutions or specific policies. Which is why there is such diffuse emotion, but also such fervor, in the people's aspirations to free themselves of foreign domination. In 1967 Israel drastically undermined these aspirations.

For the Arabs, therefore, the war of 1967 implied two things. On the one hand, it meant that they had to understand Israel, face up to it, see it as it really was; on the other hand, they had to resurrect their dignity, which Israel was trampling underfoot.

JEAN LACOUTURE: Taking off from your account, let me sum up the attitude of the Arabs in general. To the people of the Machrek—Syrians, Lebanese, Jordanians, Iraqis—Israel was a mythical monster at once very close to them and very menacing, yet not very clearly seen, a hateful source of anguish rather than a real enemy. And to the Egyptians, it was a rather remote and nebulous myth which they left up to their governments to exorcise, to annihilate.

June 1967 had two results. In the eyes of the Egyptians it transformed the distant myth into a clear and immediate threat, a wound that was deeply felt; in the eyes of Cairo

Israel became real through its very presence, through the pain it had inflicted. I hit you, therefore I am... At the same time, in the Machrek the "question of Israel" was taken over by the Palestinians, at the ideological level in any case. For the Palestinians Israel was already a very tangible reality; it could now also be viewed with some objectivity by the people in that part of the Arab world where the Hebrew state had been pictured as an inexpressible, unnameable Leviathan which it was enough not to mention to cancel out its evil-doings...

In the eyes of the Arabs, then, could the war of 1967 be defined as the "concretization," the objectification of Israel, the transformation of Israel from phantom into true enemy, the implicit acknowledgment of Israel for what it was?

MAHMOUD HUSSEIN: Yes, that's correct.

JEAN LACOUTURE: Once again, Mahmoud Hussein, I am going to try to consolidate your thoughts and simplify them so that they draw a response from Saul Friedländer, whose own version of things will no doubt be emphatically different from yours. This is how I would describe the turning point of 1967: At the very moment when the experience of being defeated and occupied finally forced the Arab world to see Israel for what it really was, to become more objective about it and move toward what could at last be the beginning of a historic dialogue, at that very moment Israel moved farther away from that dialogue and made it impossible by pursuing a dream of imperialism which started with a grandiose scheme of regional control.

In short, 1967 could be thought of as an appointment that was never kept between a group of people whose eyes had been opened to reality and another group who, at that very moment, took another way and lost themselves in dreams of glory, of becoming a superpower. For one side, defeat brought the beginning of wisdom, while for the other side victory was the beginning of a kind of madness... The good relations Arab illusions had prevented up to then were made impossible from 1967 on by the Israeli dreams of expansion...

SAUL FRIEDLÄNDER: I have said very little so far; it seemed to me that it was really up to Mahmoud Hussein to explain the shift in Arab thinking, why the dialogue that had been refused for so long was now possible. And then, too, I was trying to understand how a certain view of Israel had evolved. So far I have only managed to understand a little of this, but we have plenty of time to clarify things.

Mahmoud Hussein, I would like to try to summarize in a few sentences what I think I have grasped of your analysis. According to you, this was more or less the sequence of events: Until 1967, Israel was a frightening myth for the Machrek, and a more shadowy myth for Egypt. The war of 1967 made things more concrete, made Israel tangible and terribly present, as much for the Egyptians as for the people of the Machrek. They therefore had to ask concrete questions about Israel and think of concrete solutions. But Israel, which had become tangible and much closer than before, now seemed to grow more distant again because of its "arrogant" and "Zionist" policies. Then—if I have correctly understood the few words you said about this—the humiliation of 1967, intensified by Israeli policy in the years that followed it, was wiped out in 1973, and now the Arabs' new dignity, combined with increased awareness of Israel's concrete reality, allows the possibility of dialogue.

But what dialogue are you talking about?

I would certainly like to believe you when you say that the Arabs had no desire to exterminate the Jews. Yet you should be aware of the fact that many Israelis thought, and still think, that what the Arabs really want in the end is the extermination of the Jews. Even so, let's say you're right. It would still be true that the concrete solutions the Arabs thought of between 1967 and 1973 did not allow for the existence of a sovereign State of Israel—if I have understood you correctly—but at the very most an autonomous Jewish community within a "secular and democratic Palestine..."
I hope that in the course of the discussion this will be clarified

too... But what you say about the Arabs' point of view after
1967—which to you seemed to be a great step forward—clearly
explains the policy Israel adopted during the years that followed the
Six Day War.

For Israel, any solution which did not explicitly and
unequivocally recognize Israel as a sovereign state was obviously
unthinkable, and after the 1967 war, after the three Arab "no's" at
the Khartoum conference ("no" to recognition of Israel, "no" to
negotiation and "no" to peace), we could only conclude that
nothing had really changed and that the Arabs' ultimate goal was
still the disappearance of Israel as a sovereign state. Which was
what led the Israelis to pursue a policy which you call "arrogant"
and "Zionist" and which I would certainly call "Zionist," and
perhaps pointlessly arrogant on certain issues, and perhaps
inflexible—I wouldn't try to deny it—in the way it was expressed,
but which I would explain as the reaction to a fundamental rejection
on the part of the Arabs.

In order to understand Israel's attitude, we must try to see how
the Israelis themselves looked upon what happened and how they
reacted to it. And we are not talking only about May and June of
1967 but about the whole series of Arab threats and attempts to
destroy the State of Israel from the time it was first created. If
nothing else, a review of the historical situation will put the
attitudes of both sides into perspective.

In 1947 the United Nations decided to divide Palestine into two
states, one Jewish and the other Arab. The Arabs rejected that
decision. Beginning in November 1947, the Arabs launched a
series of attacks against the *Yishuv*, and in May 1948, when the
British mandate came to an end and the State of Israel was
proclaimed, armies from all the surrounding Arab countries joined
in the attack. Then came the armistices of 1949. The Arab
countries refused to sign the peace treaty. From the beginning of
the fifties on, groups of Arabs infiltrated and carried on sabotage in
Israeli territory, and one tends to forget that in 1955, one year
before the Sinai campaign, Nasser sent fedayeen commandos into
Israel. These fedayeen were so active and so effective that for a
time it was dangerous to travel between Tel Aviv and Jerusalem,
not to mention the constant danger that threatened the villages and
kibbutzim of the Negev. The shipments of Czech and Soviet arms

to Egypt made the Arab menace even starker. I remember that period very vividly—the anguished and fruitless appeals of Moshe Sharett (then prime minister of Israel) to the rest of the world, the participation of thousands of people in building lines of defense, at last the first shipments of arms from France. In 1955 and 1956 Israel felt that it was faced with a deadly threat.

The war of 1956 brought some respite, but in the end that respite was brief. Beginning in 1960 there were new threats, then more raids by the fedayeen, mostly from Syria, and then Jordan. There was talk of fighting us for the water of the Jordan; in other words, we lived under a constant threat.

But perhaps what mattered most had little to do with one or another specific act of sabotage, or the military threats, or the attempts to strangle Israel economically. What mattered most was that since its birth, the State of Israel had met with almost absolute rejection and hostility from the Arabs. Rejecting Israel and hostile toward it, the Arabs had not hesitated to make use of the same kinds of propaganda—ideas and writings—which the Nazis had made famous (though these writings had existed before Nazism and were in fact among the classics of European anti-Semitism). I am thinking in particular of *The Protocols of the Elders of Zion*, which was translated into Arabic several times and often quoted during the period I'm talking about.

It is within this general context that we should try to see how the Israelis perceived what happened in 1967 and reacted to it. For most of them, 1967 made a visible and tangible reality (we, too, came to see things in a most concrete way) of the Arabs' desire for the State of Israel to disappear, and I guarantee that no one saw any difference between Egypt and the Machrek—quite the contrary.

Israel has been accused of planning to attack Syria in May 1967. There was no such plan, no mobilization, nothing. These rumors were undoubtedly spread by the Russians, for reasons which are not clear even now. Be that as it may, Israel was not preparing a major attack, and yet all of a sudden, within several days, Arab hatred of extraordinary intensity was unleashed on all our borders. We had only to turn on any radio station to realize that this was a paroxysm of hatred on the mass level, not the considered expression of a few prejudiced men. . .

There might have been some Egyptians who did not want to

speak of throwing Jews into the sea, but don't forget that in May 1967 Arab radio stations were broadcasting very explicit exhortations—and I am not just referring to Shukairy, but to the Egyptians too. We really felt that a vise was closing around Israel. For the Israeli, who was completely isolated, it seemed as though the Arab vision of Israel's destiny was being realized...

At this point, war broke out. I hardly need to say that almost no one foresaw what would happen. No one in Israel thought the war would be that short and the victory that decisive. You know how the Israeli government hesitated and vacillated before June 4th; the fear was that even if Israel was not completely crushed, at the least it would be terribly weakened, which for a country of less than three million people could be fatal. In June came the astonishing victory. Then something happened which you interpreted as a sort of rush forward toward new conquests but which for most Israelis represented a completely different sequence of events: first the feeling of having escaped a terrible danger, then the desire to do everything possible to avoid the possibility of that danger ever recurring.

Of course a certain arrogance went with the victory, but any group of people would have reacted in the same way, whether it was naturally chauvinistic or not. This is unimportant compared with the intensity of Arab hatred that had just been experienced by the Israelis in a very direct and tangible way. From that moment on, their overriding concern was to make sure that in case of settlement—if settlement there had to be—the deep hatred of the Arab world for Israel would not materialize later on as an overwhelmingly serious military threat. Which is why they insisted on safe borders and were so intransigent about certain territorial matters. What seemed to you like a new rush forward was for the Israelis an elementary guarantee against recurrence of a situation that could be fatal to the very survival of the country.

You know that during this period I did not hesitate to criticize my government's policy when it seemed to me too rigid on certain points, even granted the situation I've just described. Yet no one could say this policy, whose underlying arguments I have been talking about, did not make sense. Whatever the extremists may have said—and we have our share of them—Eshkol's and Meir's governments, which succeeded one another between the war of 1967 and the war of 1973, adopted a policy which was centered around the country's basic need for security but included no intention to annex new territory just for the sake of annexing it.

JEAN LACOUTURE: Still, the "Whole Land of Israel" movement had fairly important advocates in the Israeli army and also in the political parties—the Herut, the Gahal, the Likud. Even in the government, men like Yisrael Galili, who had a big influence on Mrs. Meir and other political figures, took a very bold position in favor of annexation. It would seem that this confirms the idea put forward by Mahmoud Hussein.

SAUL FRIEDLÄNDER: Mahmoud Hussein talked about the policy of the Israeli government and characterized it as annexationist without taking the context into account—Israel's need for security in the face of permanent Arab hostility. I don't think it is necessary at this stage in the discussion to go into the details of the Israeli political scene. We will come to that eventually, just as we will be going into the details of the Egyptian political scene—at least I expect we will. So I will answer you in a fairly general way, giving the broad outlines.

Until October 1973 (after the Yom Kippur War the domestic political situation changed somewhat) there were three attitudes in Israel toward the occupied territories, and more generally, toward what the nature of a settlement would be. First of all, there was a very small group, basically composed of extreme leftists, in favor of restoring *all* occupied territories without setting any preconditions if that was the only hope for some kind of settlement. Of course, less than ten percent of the population was involved here. At the other end of the political spectrum you had a much larger group of people in favor of annexation, who were not so much interested in the Sinai as they were firmly opposed to letting any of the West Bank, part of the "historic" land of Israel, be restored to the Arabs. Beginning in 1971, most of the political figures in favor of simply annexing the West Bank found themselves back in the opposition, but I admit that the same implicit attitude could be seen in certain members of the government, and not the least important members either.

The official policy of the Israeli government never supported annexation as I have just described it. Even if on the eve of the Yom Kippur War certain pro-annexation tendencies seemed to get stronger, quite different tendencies appeared, too, and within the same political groups. You mentioned Mr. Galili. But then you ought to point out that in opposition to him there were ministers like Sapir, Allon, and Eban, not to mention more marginal but also more outspoken men like Eliav or Ben-Aharon. In any case, the official position did not change, in spite of much agitation: There could be no reversion to the borders of 4 June 1967, which were considered dangerous to the very survival of the country, nor could there be annexation of all the territories conquered in 1967.

The new borders had to run somewhere between these two lines, and the fundamental question remained the same: how to arrive at an outline for a territorial settlement that would be acceptable to the Arabs and would also provide the necessary guarantee of Israel's long-term survival. In short, how to achieve peace without sacrificing security. Obviously we interpret the policy Israel followed after the Six Day War in very different ways, and our viewpoints are equally different when we come to Egypt's position toward Israel, both well before the Six Day War and, especially, just before war broke out.

This being the case, you talked about how the Arabs, particularly the Egyptians, more or less discovered Israel's reality after June 1967. It could be said that to a certain extent the same sort of thing took place in Israel. Of course, for the Israeli the Arab problem had been the central problem right from the beginning; and I think you agree with me that there have always been more people in Israel who were well acquainted with the Arab world than there have been people in the Arab world who were experts on Israel. But for the Israeli man in the street the Arabs, too, were somewhat mythical figures before the 1967 war. He had almost no daily contacts with them except in a limited way with Arab citizens of Israel and everyone knew that these Arabs did not represent the Arab world.

The Six Day War changed all that. Whether they had wanted it or not, the Israelis found themselves coming into contact with the

Arabs of Palestine, the Arabs who lived on the West Bank. In Jerusalem Arabs walked in and out of the Jewish part of the city every day, and Jews in and out of the Arab part. There were contacts, then, first in Jerusalem where the two populations had mingled since the end of the fighting, then on the whole of the West Bank. I can point to my own experience as an example. I go to the West Bank fairly often. I have been in the market at Hebron, and it is a rather dark, dangerous looking labyrinth; but I did not feel I had anything to be afraid of, and I think that this is the attitude of most Israelis. The same is true for Arab inhabitants of Jerusalem, the West Bank, or Gaza. They come to the Jewish part of Jerusalem or go to Tel Aviv and other parts of Israel to work or shop without being afraid they are going to be lynched in the street or even insulted by anyone. At that level the two populations have intermingled enough for the Israeli to come to know the Arab—the Arab as a man, the everyday, ordinary Arab who drinks coffee with you, argues with you, with whom you finally discover the possibility of coexisting. In this sense, there is a resemblance.

Since 1948 the Arab danger has been concrete, and it remains so for the Israeli, but he did not discover the Arab as a neighbor until 1967. The Israelis have always spoken of dialogue, but perhaps that dialogue was to take place with rather mythical Arabs, and here I agree with you. Israelis were not quite sure how to carry on a dialogue with a real Arab. Two parallel tendencies are clearly evident today, but the problem is to know whether we are going to arrive at a sufficiently objective view of one another for the dialogue that takes place not to be a dialogue between deaf people. This is the crucial point we have arrived at now. Let's take an example, to put the difficulty into concrete terms. When you implied that Israel was making dialogue impossible because of the fact that since 1967 it had become in some way more and more "Zionist," you were implicitly suggesting, it seemed to me, that dialogue and contact would have been possible if Israel had been revolutionary and not Zionist. But you should be aware that for all Israelis—apart from the partisans of Rakah or Matzpen—*there is no such thing as a "non-Zionist Israel."* The notion is even contradictory in itself, and represents a totally distorted image of the true Israel.

JEAN LACOUTURE: I would like to raise one objection to that. Five years ago we published a book by our friend Uri Avnery called *Israel Without Zionism*, which asserts—whatever you might think of this—that the hypothesis can at least be entertained...

SAUL FRIEDLÄNDER: Avnery represents almost nothing, at least in Israel...

Two Unyielding Points of View

JEAN LACOUTURE: We have heard parallel descriptions of two stages of history which the Arabs and the Israelis passed through during the last twenty-five years. Before 1967 was the period of mythology and nonrecognition; from 1967 to 1973 gradual recognition intensified the basic hostility; and now, after 1973, we have reached another stage. Perhaps Mahmoud Hussein could tell us how the elements of the problem changed drastically enough to open the Arab people to the idea of holding a dialogue.

MAHMOUD HUSSEIN: The beginning of our dialogue—which until now has really consisted of two monologues—shows very clearly that before 1973 the Arabs and the Israelis formed two universes that were closed to one another. On each side, of course, there were groups that tried to understand the other better, but circumstances prevented these groups from finding common ground.

The standards by which events were judged were too dissimilar, and the balance of power was too unequal for the situation really to change without a complete reversal of the conditions created by the 1967 war. This reversal did not occur until 1973.

One example will be enough to show that any discussion taking place before then would have been futile. Friedländer has just told us that in the years 1955 and 1956 the Israelis felt they were in mortal danger. Why? Because Nasser, whose regime had barely started to take shape, had just received his first modern weapons from Eastern Europe—several dozen tanks and airplanes destined for an army which had only recently come into being. A small thing, really, which the Arabs saw as the very first step toward true independence. But the Israeli leaders saw it as a mortal threat.

At first sight, the Israeli fears you have been talking about seem to me rather morbid. Of course, on closer examination there is much more to them than that. This divergence of viewpoints epitomizes all the antagonistic feelings of the two countries. Israel felt safe only to the degree that the Arabs were powerless and resembled the image which Europeans had had of them at the beginning of the century. Israel's original sin, of having been conceived in colonialist Europe, expressed itself in a frame of reference that was totally foreign to the national Arab movement's frame of reference.

The Israelis' ideological frame of reference was rooted in the West. Within this framework, the Jews related Israel to Czarist or Nazi Europe rather than to the Arab world. It was the Jews' answer to the pogroms and the gas chambers. The memories, the hopes, the struggles of the Jews before 1948 created a system of values whose criteria were not grounded in the Arab world, where the Jews were settling, but in Europe.

That is why the Israelis, in the end, were incapable of seeing, or in any case interpreting, the profound meaning of Arab national aspirations. All they saw was a challenge to their own odyssey and they translated that challenge into the terms of their own mythology. For them the Arabs were the reincarnation of the Nazis, Nasser was potentially a smaller version of Hitler, the immense wave of enthusiasm felt by the people after the nationalization of the Suez Canal was a deathly vise tightening around the survivors of Auschwitz. No one should be surprised if to the Arabs Israel remained a foreign intruder.

SAUL FRIEDLÄNDER: I think that this morning we are already approaching the heart of the debate. Two attitudes toward the immediate situation are coming into conflict, as we have just said, and they are offshoots of views of history which themselves go back to a distant but traumatic past.

I am going to come to the Jewish point of view in a minute, but I would like to say what I think of your point of view, since you have just told me how the link between Israel and Jewish history should be understood. Again there are parallels.

You spoke of the link between present-day Israel and Jewish history, particularly in Europe, but we should also be aware of the link between your perception of Israel and your experience of the colonial presence. You have been subjected to colonial humiliation, persecution, the Western presence—both French and English—and you believe that Israel, which you see as an emanation, an extension of the West, really is the continuation (or the voice, or the tool, or the servant) of Western imperialism. You, the Arabs, have a certain explicit or implicit vision of the past—you see a period of glory being followed by a period of decadence and humiliation, which in turn is supposed to lead into a period of rebirth and renewal. These three stages are clearly recognizable in the way the Islamic world sees itself. Obviously the European imperialist powers (and the United States) are considered the main causes of the decadence and humiliation.

According to you, Israel came and set itself up in the very middle of this phase of humiliation. I understand your logic: In order for you to arrive at the third period, in other words the return to the glorious past, Israel would have to disappear, since both locally and historically, as you see it, Israel represents the most concrete and most immediate expression of the complex and diffuse force of Western imperialism.

MAHMOUD HUSSEIN: I don't want to simplify anything. Not at all. I want to look at all aspects of the problem without denying the many things that have changed, from the Jews' point of view, since they first had their own state. It is clear, now, that to them this represented a regeneration, a new achievement, a reaffirmation of dignity which perhaps the Arabs can understand better than anyone else. But at the same time I would like to show that this process took place in a different context from the one in which the dream of Zionism was born.

This context was the Arab Middle East, the system of imperialist domination set up by the French and English here, and the fervent patriotism of the Arabs, who were beginning to fight this system. The Zionist project, with all its idealism, was introduced into this reality. There was no way it could change the way things were. It had to define its place within a preexisting situation, and it chose to side with the oppressors.

We should therefore try to agree on this fact, which is as much beyond your control as it is beyond ours. The way the Arabs saw Zionism was subjective, unrealistic, simplified, but they intuitively felt their judgment was correct. The Zionists had joined the ranks of the enemies of the Arab national movement.

SAUL FRIEDLÄNDER: You are emphasizing something which I think is of secondary importance while failing to see what appears to me most important about Zionism—the constant, living bond between the Jewish people and the land of Israel throughout Jewish history.

The fact that England played a part in the return of the Jews to Palestine after the First World War seems to me a minor detail in the end. We are now aware that instead of the Balfour Declaration there could have been a declaration of the same kind by Germany or even by France, depending on the circumstances. In any case, even as an organized political movement Zionism preceded the Balfour Declaration by more than twenty years, and as a deep aspiration it preceded the declaration by nineteen centuries. If Zionism were nothing more than the ephemeral product of a contemporary situation in Europe, it would be a movement which I do not think I would want to be connected with and which most Israelis would not consider to be something permanent. Try to follow me, even if you don't agree. If you cannot understand that Zionism is the result of an aspiration that is literally almost two thousand years old, then you cannot understand anything about Israel, about its will, its tenacity. You will not be able to understand anything about it if you don't see what its true roots are.

You probably know that up to the end of the nineteenth century most Jews were practicing Jews. Eretz Yisrael (the land of Israel) was the very center of their thoughts and their prayers. As a matter of fact, the Russian Jew, for example, as he trembled with cold in his village in White Russia, would pray for rain in the middle of winter because his "real" frame of reference was Palestine. But even the nonpracticing Jews, the Jews of today, speak of "next year in Jerusalem."

You probably know that from time immemorial elderly Jews have hoped to die in Palestine and have tried to make their way back there. Messianic movements of return did spring up from time to time—the most famous was Sabbatai Zevi's—when thousands of Jews sold everything they had, closed their shops, and left for Palestine. I could give more examples, but one thing is clear: Jewish identity is a function of the awareness of the bond with the land of Israel. Not that this shouldn't be seen within the contemporary political context—of course it should—but what is essential for you is only an accident of circumstances for me. Perhaps it would have been harder for Zionism to fulfill itself outside these circumstances, but its drive, its tenacity, its strength, can only be explained by its own deep roots.

MAHMOUD HUSSEIN: I am aware of the fact that Zionism was the answer to an aspiration on the part of the people. And quite apart from what I think of that answer, I see that it carried the hopes, the dreams, the demands of the people without which the Zionist project, even backed by a great power, would not have been able to survive in the heart of an Arab world which was natually hostile to it. But even so, that does not reduce its alliance with the colonial powers to simple happenstance.

The State of Israel is the product of that alliance. It is made up of two elements: Jewish aspiration and an imperialist plan. It would have been doomed in advance if the Jewish pioneers had not been assured of British protection between the two world wars. That protection was essential to them, and its importance cannot be diminished by saying that it was not unconditional.

You say the Balfour Declaration was only an accident of circumstance. By that you mean that in other circumstances the declaration could have been signed by the Kaiser or by President Wilson. But that still doesn't take us outside the bounds of the great powers who are competing for control of the Middle Eastern nations. For the Zionist leaders, there was no question of tying the fate of their movement to the fate of the Arab anti-imperialist movement. This is the heart of the problem.

If we insist on that here today, it is because that "accident of circumstance" has a decisive bearing on Israel's present position in the Middle East. Until today Israel has kept its face turned toward the sea, toward the West. England's protection, which began to falter at the end of the thirties, was replaced after a fashion by American support following the Second World War, for a short time by Russian aid, then by French, English, and German help, and finally by American protection again—which was going to end up being as possessive as it was intrusive. The development of Israel was constantly identified with some imperialist presence.

SAUL FRIEDLÄNDER: But tell me, wasn't Arab nationalism born under exactly the same circumstances? Who was involved in the beginnings of Arab nationalism? It was the British and the French. It was with them, or against them, setting one against the other, that Arab nationalism finally asserted itself. And even today, don't the Arabs depend partly on the Soviet Union and partly on aid from the United States? What we really have here are two profoundly motivated movements, which within a dramatic set of circumstances are finding their political expression at the same time. They are using or being used by what we would agree to call imperialist forces, and for this reason are caught in the crosscurrents of world politics. Obviously they cannot control these politics, but neither did these politics create them.

MAHMOUD HUSSEIN: No, not at all. There is a sizeable difference between our appraisals of the two situations. You may have noticed that I have not spoken of the nationalist movement but of the Arab national movement, in which the nationalist impulse is only one element and reflects the bourgeois or petit bourgeois attitude toward the national question.

In contemporary Arab history, nationalism is an ambiguous movement. It embodies both a widespread aspiration toward dignity and independence and the interest of a privileged class in establishing its own power over society. This class is usually somewhat inconspicuous when compared to the popular base of the national movement, whose diffuse aspirations are more radical, more anti-imperialist, and are often expressed by autonomous revolts which the nationalist leaders try to channel elsewhere, or retrieve, or sometimes suppress. So the national movement and the nationalist trend within that movement should not be confused.

Now, to the extent, even to the limited extent, that this trend embodies the wider aspirations of the national movement during a particular period of history, it represents a force that opposes imperialist domination, a force that participates, in a more or less inconsequential way, in challenging that domination.

Zionist nationalism developed in exactly the opposite way. For the Zionist leaders—and the most important of them, Weizmann* and Ben-Gurion, clearly spelled it out—the implantation of the Jewish national homeland was bound in with the perpetuation of imperialist domination. Weizmann even said explicitly that the homeland should be a bastion of the West against the mounting national movement in the region. The difference between the two nationalisms, therefore, is not superficial.

Arab nationalism wanted to do as much as possible, within the relatively narrow framework of class interests, to weaken the imperialist presence in the region. Zionist nationalism wanted—and still wants—just the opposite, to prevent that weakening, because the imperialist presence constitutes the only possible foundation for the presence of Israel itself.

SAUL FRIEDLÄNDER: I don't agree with your analysis of the situation. You are simply underestimating the true foundations of Zionism. You still have a tendency, and it's quite understandable, to associate Zionism with its Western "protectors." Yet Zionism soon found itself isolated from its "protectors" and opposed to them, England being the first. As early as the twenties, the English started going back on the promises they made in the Balfour Declaration—I'm sure you are aware that in 1922 they sliced off three-quarters of the part of Palestine they had promised to the Jews in order to form Transjordan (this was Churchill's doing). Then,

*Chaim Weizmann, one of the founders of the Zionist movement and an internationally famous chemist. He was the first president of the State of Israel.

starting in 1929, they made a series of decisions that were more and more distressing to the *Yishuv* and ended in 1939 with Chamberlain's famous White Paper, which came at a moment when the Zionist movement had greatest need of England's support. The doors of Palestine were closed and immigration was halted just when the world war and the extermination of European Jews were beginning. At that point the Zionist movement found itself totally isolated, against England; Chamberlain's White Paper became a death warrant for Zionism, at the very moment when Nazi Germany had actually decided to put the Jews to death. In the Arab world during these same years, there were men—I am not speaking of the masses, because who knows what they were thinking, but of the bourgeoisie, to adopt your terms—there were men who formed alliances with the English, or in certain circumstances—Rashid Ali and others, for example—with the Germans or the Italians. So that you had solid connections with the great European powers. Which was quite understandable.

At the end of the war, the French and the English were quickly displaced from the Middle East, and we witnessed penetration by America and then by Russia. There again, the situation of the Jews and the situation of the Arabs were not entirely dissimilar, at least not in the beginning.

Starting in 1945, the Zionist movement and the *Yishuv*, in other words the Jewish community in Palestine, came into direct conflict with England and turned to Truman and America for support. That lasted for several years, in fact until the Republicans came into office in the United States; the period of the Eisenhower administration marked a certain cooling off of American-Israeli relations. As for the Arab world, it was directly supported by England in the 1947–1948 fighting (Glubb Pasha was an English officer). Then came the gradual breaking of ties with the English, their departure from Egypt, the expulsion of Glubb from Jordan, but also, at the same time, relations were established between certain Arab countries and the United States, and the Soviet Union stepped into the region as the "protector" of Egypt and Syria. You might say, of course, that as a socialist power the Soviet Union cannot be put on the same footing as the United States, but the ideological tags do not change the situation. My argument, unlike yours, at least so far, is that the two movements found themselves in tragically similar situations. Modern Arab nationalism has very deep roots, and Zionism, which is the expression of Jewish nationalism, does too. But the two movements were caught, in the same way and at the same time, in the rivalry of powers trying to use them in identical ways.

JEAN LACOUTURE: Perhaps it would be interesting to recall that after the Second World War the Soviet government was anxious to find out which of the two movements was more progressive (or more useful to Russian interests)—Zionism or the Arab movement. For a while in the beginning, Stalin and his ministers backed Zionism, alleging that the Arab movement was a tool of English imperialism.

In 1947 Moscow solemnly declared itself in favor of the partition that produced the State of Israel. During the summer of 1948 the endangered *Haganah* was saved by a shipment of Czech arms—actually Russian arms. Were the Marxists being misled? Critical as Mahmoud Hussein might be of Stalin, this is an interesting indication of the way Moscow viewed Zionism.

MAHMOUD HUSSEIN: Stalin's decision, Gromyko's speech, and the shipping of Czech arms to the Zionists at the time of the first armistice came from an assessment I obviously don't feel tied to at all. And the quick reversal of the USSR's position on these questions shows clearly—if this must indeed be shown—that it had not taken that position out of principle. Nowhere in any of those theoretical documents—which the Soviets publish in such great numbers on subjects they feel strongly about—have I found an explanation of the precise reason for their support of the Zionists, support which turned into overt hostility within a few years.

Rather, I think this was a political tactic, an attempt to gain a foothold, since England was beginning to withdraw from the region and at that time the United States had only taken its first steps there. Perhaps there was also some selfish motive connected with the Jewish problem in the USSR itself.

Right now, for example, China—which in the past took a very

outspoken stand on the Middle East—had adopted an attitude that is much more subtle. If my information is correct, this is part of a policy which consists of opposing the growing Soviet influence everywhere and supporting even the bastions of American influence. But you will probably agree that these considerations do not advance our own debate at all. So perhaps it is time to return to that debate.

In Friedländer's account of the Zionist movement, in the parallels he tried to establish between Zionist nationalism and Arab nationalism, I can see the basic difference between us. I can see that his vision of things is rooted in the West, where Zionism was born, and that this prevents him from perceiving the difference between the two forms of nationalism. From the Zionist point of view, the great Western powers did not constitute a strange and alienating reality; they were simply the leaders of the Western universe, of which Israel was also an integral part. What Israel did was to profit by what each of these powers could contribute and eventually to make use of their quarrels to gain a certain freedom to act autonomously. But there was no question of Israel placing itself beyond the area the Western powers controlled, of dissociating itself totally from them, of challenging the Western presence in the Middle East. Quite the opposite. Israel wanted to help strengthen that presence in every way—because Zionism was organically linked to it.

Arab nationalism, in spite of the opportunism and cowardice of its various spokesmen, considers the West a foreigner, a conqueror; its presence in our midst is humiliating, provoking, debilitating. The more the Arabs succeed in shaking and weakening that presence, the more truly they have reaffirmed themselves. And their nationalist leaders, even the least important of them, have tried as far as possible, each in his own way, to challenge that presence. In attempting to gain from the rivalries among the great powers, a man like Nasser was not in the same position as a man like Ben-Gurion. According to Ben-Gurion, the point was for Israel to profit as much as possible while at the same time strengthening Western influence in the Middle East. In Nasser's eyes, the point was to weaken that influence and thereby strengthen an Arab nation that was just coming into existence.

SAUL FRIEDLÄNDER: The same image of Zionism keeps recurring. For us Zionism is not a movement that came in from outside and grew in opposition to the local population, but a movement of return based on the strong bond between the Jewish people and the land of Israel. The objective of Zionism was not to displace the inhabitants of Palestine.

Actually everything you say about Zionism is exactly what Zionism has never wanted to be, but has perhaps been forced to become as a consequence of the Arabs' own intransigence, particularly that of the Palestinians...

October 1973: A New Era?

JEAN LACOUTURE: Bearing in mind these historical elements—social, psychological, even emotional—we can begin to approach the heart of the matter—the impact of the October 1973 war. In what way, Mahmoud Hussein, did it transform the elements of the situation?

MAHMOUD HUSSEIN: The most important fact in 1973 was that the Arab armies were waging a real war. The main army, the Egyptian army, had not really seen action either in 1967 or in 1956. It had been taken by surprise and defeated twice before it actually had a chance to fight. In 1948 it wasn't a national army in the true sense of the word. It consisted of eighteen thousand men whose arms supply was controlled by the English.

In point of fact, when you think about it, the last battles fought by a real Egyptian army were in the time of Mohammed Ali in the middle of the nineteenth century. This should give some indication of how important October 1973 was for reasserting the nation's dignity. The details of troop movements, the degree of technical mastery of the new weapons, the exact relations between the forces at the time of the cease-fire are minor matters compared to this new psychological element—the conviction that from then on Arab armies were capable of fighting real battles. Weakness, carelessness, lack of preparation were no longer second nature, defeat was no longer inevitable.

Even if the Arab armies are defeated now and then in the future, they have proved that at least a series of victories—if not the definitive victory—is possible. With time, space, and numbers in their favor, they can now regard the future with new confidence. The horizon of the Arab people is no longer darkened by the immense shadow of the Israeli army; they can breathe again; they can even think of things other than war.

SAUL FRIEDLÄNDER: But how is the transition made from the situation that existed between 1967 and 1973 to concrete recognition of Israel, and then to the idea of dialogue?

MAHMOUD HUSSEIN: Please be patient. The idea of dialogue could only come into being in a certain context—and this context is exactly what is so difficult to describe, because there are many elements in it which are both interdependent and contradictory at the same time.

Until 1973 the Arabs' more or less outright recognition of Israel's reality had been expressed in a rather contradictory form; they wanted to measure themselves against it and define themselves in relation to it. Then from the moment they were free of the obsession with 1967, and could get beyond the feeling of being permanently disabled that defeat had given them, they were able to express their recognition of Israel in other ways.

There is no longer any question that Israel as an entity will remain; the question is rather how Israel can be introduced into the Arab context in a way that will be acceptable to the Arabs. For some the answer would be long-term settlement with the Zionist institution itself; for others that would be a beginning, but since institutional Zionism is tied too organically to the imperialist West to be able to adapt itself to the Arab national context, it would be necessary later for the forces of change among the Arabs and Israelis to recognize one another and work together to challenge both Zionism and the larger system of foreign domination.

We will certainly be coming back to this point, but the essential

fact is that after October 1973, the various large movements in
Arab thought—which differ from one another on vital
points—could at last pose the problem of relations with Israel on a
realistic basis rather than on a mythical basis. There might be war
or there might be peace, but either one would be with a real, flesh
and blood Israel.

JEAN LACOUTURE: Could we say that the 1967 war proved to
the Arabs that Israel existed and that in an almost symmetrical
way the 1973 war proved to the Arabs that they themselves
existed? This is the point where we reach the prospect of
dialogue. Before 1967 Israel was a myth, after 1967 it was
real; before 1973 the Arabs were a sort of myth in their own
eyes, and after 1973 they rediscovered and recognized their
own existence. The two operations complement one another
in much the same way that two images come into focus in an
optical instrument. . .

SAUL FRIEDLÄNDER: Perhaps it would be helpful now to see how
Israel experienced these same events. As I have already said, Israel
was always ready for dialogue. The Six Day War and the contact
which followed it with Arabs from the West Bank brought the
Arabs closer and made the possibility of exchanges more likely.
After this, in October 1973, came the attack by the Egyptians and
the Syrians. The Israelis experienced the war of 1973 as a very
dramatic occurrence. They were still ready to enter into a dialogue,
but they were more worried than they had been before, and I think I
should elaborate certain points that I've already made in connection
with this. If the Israelis' uneasiness is not understood, there will be
another break and another war. And who knows how that might
end?

I have already said this morning that the Israelis' deepest worry
is that some day they will find themselves as a group face to face
with a danger they will be unable to fend off. When you were
recalling how the Israelis reacted to the rearmament of Egypt in
1955 and 1956, Mahmoud Hussein, you said that these reactions
were the result of a morbid fear. It is not morbid. What we are
talking about here is a real experience of rejection, isolation, and

persecution, the Israeli experience coming on top of the Jewish experience. And in order to be sure you understand what I mean, I would like to say a few words about that Jewish experience, which you yourself have mentioned.

I think it is safe to say that the whole of Jewish history has been one long experience of persecution and loneliness. Perhaps this has not always been true for the Jew as an individual, but it is certainly true for the Jews as a community. The reasons for this situation do not concern us here. A discussion of them would lead us far astray. But it is no less true, and just as clear as the situation itself, that until the twentieth century the Jew did not believe that persecution would end in the total destruction of the people of Israel. I do not think I am wrong in suggesting that this certainty disappeared at the time of the Second World War, when the European Jews were being exterminated.

One absolutely must not underestimate the importance of the Holocaust and its decisive effect on the minds of both the Jews of the Diaspora and the Israelis (including the generation that hadn't been born at the time). I have had my students at the University of Jerusalem carry out inquiries to see how much the European Holocaust has marked Israeli thinking in its most concrete manifestations—in its foreign policy and its military policy, and particularly at the level of the thinking of its leaders. The influence is profound. What 1967 meant was the possibility of another Auschwitz. You ask me, Mahmoud Hussein, "Isn't it morbid?" My answer is, "No, it comes from the weight of experience, the past, history." Also, you keep forgetting the true dimensions of the problem. As an Egyptian, as an Arab, if I may venture to say this, you are speaking in the name of a very large community of people. You really know very well that whatever Israel might do, it could not conquer the Arab world. Israel could win one battle, ten battles, it could advance and retreat but that's all it could do.

Before we began our debate, we were talking about Cairo. You mentioned that Cairo had eight million inhabitants; if this goes on for another year or two, it will have three times the population of Israel. You forget the dimensions we are talking about. You forget that when it was created in 1948, the Jewish state had all together six hundred thousand inhabitants.

MAHMOUD HUSSEIN: If you will allow me a short interruption, the concrete aspect of the problem cannot be reduced to a matter of numbers. Numbers are important but never decisive. During the thirties Japan occupied China, even though China had seven or eight times as many people; during the last century England, which is a small island, carved out an empire on which the sun never set.

In these cases the vital difference between the oppressor and the oppressed was the difference in military strength, which in turn resulted from economic potentials that were qualitatively different. The Israelis have certainly always relied on this sort of inequality, and more than ever since 1967.

We should not forget that certain leaders declared that the Israeli army was capable of intervening anywhere in the Arab world, from Baghdad to Algiers. And when the "Arabologists" in Washington and Tel Aviv are asked what balance of military strength would be ideal in the Middle East, they say very explicitly that Israel should remain stronger than all its neighbors combined. Under these circumstances, there is no need to occupy the Arab world; Israel can impose its will by the very fact of its being so strong. You must admit that numbers do not seem to matter in this case.

SAUL FRIEDLÄNDER: If I manage, today, to explain to you how I see things (explain, not convince...), I think we will have made immense progress, and not only in the shaping of this book. You see the Israelis as people who are "sure of themselves and domineering,"* who want to assert themselves by force, keep others under their yoke with an army that is technologically very advanced. But the Israelis simply fear for their survival. They are not sure that no matter what happens things will work out. After October 1973 they were even less sure than before—not because they have less confidence in themselves but because they see the beginning of a certain change. This is why they demand so many guarantees and take such care over the smallest details relating to their safety. You say that numbers do not matter, you make a comparison with Japan and China. All the same, we are dealing with other proportions here!

*This quotation refers to a statement about Israel made by General DeGaulle in November 1967.

Until 1973 Israel was able to say: "We must take Arab hostility into account, but can hold our own because for the moment the disparity in technological development is in our favor, which gives us a certain margin of safety." I think this was not as clear after October 1973. If nothing else, the Yom Kippur War showed that the Egyptians and the Syrians could use modern equipment effectively. Israel is therefore in danger of losing its technological advantage, and numbers could then well become a decisive factor. Obviously this situation should make Israel uneasy. And you cannot dismiss this uneasiness out of hand. Nor can you say: "Trust us, the future will take care of itself." Even if you yourselves were convinced of it, you could not ask the Israelis to say all right, we'll trust you without too many guarantees, and we'll see what happens. I think 1973 increased a constant anxiety which may have been somewhat relieved by the situation that existed immediately after the Six Day War, but which was very deep.

MAHMOUD HUSSEIN: I can imagine what anxiety the Israelis must have felt at various times, including June 1967, even if I don't see the objective reasons for the anxiety. This is another example of your tendency to interpret what goes on in the Middle East in terms of Europe and the gas chambers.

But the anxiety you speak of does not always have the same weight, the same substance. It certainly subsided a great deal after 1967, and was gradually replaced by confidence and tranquility. But even so, unfortunately, this did not lead most Israelis to see their relations with the Arabs in a new light; it did not lead to greater understanding of the Arabs, more restraint towards them, a deeper sense of their most important aspirations. On the contrary, it led to more arrogance, more shortsightedness.

Why? Undoubtedly because the Israeli leaders did not feel any anxiety in 1967. As certain Israeli generals admitted later, the leaders were well aware of the relative strengths of the military forces; and immediately after the war, they started to widen the scope of their ambitions. The most influential among them, at least, began to appreciate their new conquests and the extraordinarily strong position they held because of those conquests.

Then they tried to force the hand of the Arab people, to wrest from them an admission of weakness, seen as the condition for Israel's safety.

But by insisting on new security frontiers, the Israeli leaders extended the frontiers of the problem. They blocked all possibility of a meeting between the two sides, and widened the gap that separated them. Nearly everyone in Israel left everything up to the leaders and contented himself with the mistaken impression that after 1967 the Arabs would finally resign themselves to the conditions laid down by Golda Meir's government. There was a great deal of equivocation there, and it is not surprising that under the circumstances the Arab people, who had been deeply hurt, were not inclined to appreciate the extent of the Israelis' anxiety.

What they did see, on the other hand, was the annexation of certain recently occupied territories, Israelis settling on the Golan Heights—for good, as they declared over and over again—the economic integration of the West Bank with Israel through the establishment of more and more *nachalim*,* which served as Jewish population centers in Palestinian territory, the dissolution of Arab Jerusalem amid the new Jewish quarters that surrounded the city, the exploitation of Egyptian oil taken from the Sinai, all this and then, on top of it, as if to irritate public feeling even more, the attention that was drawn to the arrival of tens of thousands of Jewish immigrants coming from the USSR—more scholars, more technicians, more pilots, to reinforce the occupying force which seemed more and more permanent.

The Zionist plan for a greater Israel, one which would stretch from the Nile to the Euphrates and unite all the Jews in the world, was taking shape before our eyes, trampling on Egyptian and Syrian sovereignty, mocking Palestinian hopes for national rebirth, threatening the whole of the Arab world with a cyclical Israeli expansion that would keep pace with the needs of the accelerated immigration. This is what the Arab world saw between 1967 and 1973.

SAUL FRIEDLÄNDER: We decided we wouldn't keep returning to the past, but even so, I think we have to clear up certain problems, if

---

*Military-agricultural settlements.

only to be able to understand what is happening now and what is in danger of happening in the near future.

First I would like to respond to an idea which follows implicitly from what you are saying, namely that it would be easier for Israel to bring over and absorb millions of Jews within the frontiers established after the war of 1967 than within the frontiers that existed before it. This isn't accurate. Before his death Ben-Gurion gave a remarkable interview over Israeli television which was very much commented upon, and which was shown several times. In this interview he said that Israel had to give back to the Arabs almost all the territories occupied in 1967. When he was asked, "But where are we going to put all our immigrants?" he answered, "In the Negev." Serious people in Israel definitely do not think that more land is necessary to accommodate the immigrants. The Japanese know very well now how possible it is to achieve a very high level of development, numerically and qualitatively, within a very limited area. Most Israelis know it too.

Let's return to what could have been done in 1967. Steps were taken, but even though they were mentioned later, no one seems to know of them: In June of 1967—either the end of June or the beginning of July—the Israeli government, which was then a coalition government and included such men as Begin, leader of the extreme nationalist right wing, decided to use America as intermediary to let Egypt know that Israel was ready to restore the Sinai in exchange for a peace settlement. Presumably the American government transmitted Israel's offer. What was the answer? The three "no's" at Khartoum. The Israeli government then reversed its decision and adopted a policy which did not change afterwards, and which is still its policy, even after the war of 1973: not to return to the 1967 borders but to form defensible borders lying somewhere between those of before and after the war. This is the policy I've already described to you, and it goes on to say that while Israel will not dramatically restore all the territories acquired during the 1967 war, it will not annex all of them either.

But in that case, you will ask, why the establishment of military kibbutzim and even some civilian groups on the Golan Heights and the West Bank, and so forth? There are two attitudes towards this—the attitude taken by the partisans of annexation, whom I've already talked about and who are in the opposition, and the attitude of the government (before 1973). That attitude could be defined this way: Since a peace treaty was hardly foreseeable in the near future, Israel set itself up in these new positions so it could wait. There was no question of their being permanent positions. I can cite General Dayan himself, and he was not considered very flexible on this subject. He expressed himself clearly: Let us establish agricultural colonies so we can wait—or, in his own words, "to get a little breathing room." He believed we would have to wait a long time—and we always come back to the same idea—because the Arabs would take a long time to accept the existence of Israel. We did not know if they ever would. But supposing they did, the resulting agreement would have to be destined to last.

There would also be some kind of coexistence with the Arabs of the West Bank, an economic interdependence. Whatever happens afterwards, said Dayan, this coexistence must remain. Transcending the borders which separate one country from another, there must be economic integration of the region, the only solution that promotes long-term peace for the future.

To sum up, from the very beginning Israel's deepest, most basic concern has been the safety of the people, the survival of the state. The war of 1967 only made that concern more acute, because of the events that led up to the war. After the war, the government secretly offered the restitution of the Sinai—I don't remember about the other areas (perhaps the Golan Heights were involved too)—in exchange for a formal peace treaty. There was no response to this proposal. Then the Israeli government modified its position—which has remained the same ever since—and based it on the following points: The country must have defensible frontiers, not those dating from the June 1967 victory but ones which would lie between them and the borders that existed before June 4th. As long as the Arabs do not agree to a real peace treaty—and we mean a peace treaty, not some sort of precarious arrangement—Israel will remain, waiting expectantly, in its present territorial position, not out of any desire for annexation but for fear of losing territories which Israel considers (rightly or wrongly) to be essential pledges or guarantees of its safety.

MAHMOUD HUSSEIN: This presentation of the facts shows how differently things were viewed by each side. Israel's proposal to return the Sinai should be seen within the context of the time. The proposal was apparently addressed only to Egypt. The rest of the occupied Arab territories—and the West Bank in particular—were ignored. The plan was clear—its aim was to separate Nasser from the other Arab leaders and divide the Arab forces that were confronting Israel. Would Nasser be likely to find it acceptable? I should think definitely not.

Nasser was not against a negotiated settlement, quite the contrary—even after the summit conference at Khartoum. This was made very clear two months later when he accepted the Security Council's Resolution 242 of November 22nd. Later, Sadat went even further, and some of his proposals—particularly the proposal to reopen the Suez Canal as the first step toward a complete settlement—were found humiliating by part of the Arab population. Yet the Israelis refused all these advances.

We remember one of Dayan's statements in which he accused the United States of being in too much of a hurry to arrive at a compromise which would be acceptable to Sadat. Essentially, he felt that there was no hurry, since the Israeli army was invulnerable and its positions ideal. He felt it would be better to wait until the Arabs yielded to Israel's demands for direct negotiations without preliminaries, in other words, until the Arabs accepted the premise that Israel would annex certain of the territories occupied in 1967, and until they gave up the idea of making Israel recognize the Palestinians' right to national status. It would be better to wait for the Arabs to capitulate, an idea which was all the more attractive to the Americans since it meant a failure for Soviet diplomacy.

It also seems clear that the United States allowed itself to be won over to this point of view. This was certainly the growing conviction among Arabs—Israel and the United States were not waiting for the Arabs to try to be realistic, but for the collapse of all resistance on their part. Abba Eban, then minister of foreign affairs, was already saying that the quality of the peace would depend on how much the Arab frontiers opened for economic exchange with Israel.

So it is true that Israel's plan was not to keep most of the occupied territory, but rather to use it as bargaining money to obtain as many political and economic concessions as possible from the Arabs. For us it was the very principle of this haggling, which made our territories the barter, that was intolerable. Yet since 1967 the Israelis had been playing this game, and they played it not only with us but in their strategic relations with Washington.

In this context the Israeli leaders could not help but be infected by megalomania. You quoted Ben-Gurion before his death; what he said is not convincing. Israeli politicians took him for an eccentric character at that time. He had not been involved with them for several years, and as a group they did not share his views on the future. The very fact that his interviewer asked him the question clearly shows that the relation between territorial expansion and immigration naturally occurred to Israelis at the time.

In any case, the unofficial proposal made to Nasser after the war of 1967 cannot be connected with Ben-Gurion's last statements, which came out of a different state of mind. As far as I can see, that proposal could only have been a device of some kind—unless it was an indication of unexpected naiveté on the part of the Israeli leaders—because it would have been impossible after the Arab defeat for Nasser to agree to a transaction which consisted of taking back the Sinai while abandoning the Arab part of Jerusalem, the West Bank, and the Golan Heights to their fate. Any intelligent Israeli can understand that.

It would be ridiculous to think that this proposal encouraged any sort of dialogue. Everything that happened afterward showed this. The successive proposals of Nasser and of Sadat, even those of Hussein of Jordan—and God knows they were con- ciliatory—remained dead letters. The Israeli leaders refused to ac- knowledge the principle of return of all the occupied territories as a basis for negotiations. They thus forced the Arab leaders, even the most moderate of them, to a crisis which could have no outcome other than war.

A New Spirit on Both Sides?

JEAN LACOUTURE: You started telling us, Mahmoud Hussein, how that war changed the Arabs' point of view, particularly by giving them the feeling that they had recovered their dignity. Could we take it from there, and try to define the new spirit which from 1973 on led to the possibility of dialogue?

MAHMOUD HUSSEIN: October 1973 allowed the Arabs to think in a concrete way about the problems which were arising between Israel as a political fact and the Arab community, no longer ashamed of itself. The Arabs were not trying to exorcise the demons of the past now; they were trying to resolve real contradictions.

On the other hand, the arrogance of some of the Israelis and the sleepy complacency of others gave way suddenly to a feeling of surprise at seeing that the Arabs had emerged from the Middle Ages, where they had seemed content to stay and where most Israelis had consigned them with a certain scorn, as Friedländer himself said. They began to move, they advanced, they changed the nature of a relationship which had begun to seem inviolable; a great many Israelis had to begin to envisage a relationship with the Arab world other than one of military competition, because from then on, time was going to be on the side of the Arabs.

The anxiety that had existed before 1967 undoubtedly surfaced again. No one in Israel was sure of anything any more, now that the supremacy of the army—on which all hopes for the future had rested—had been challenged, and would remain in question for an indefinite length of time to come. Arabs and Israelis would now be on the same wavelength. But we must be careful, here, because the situation created by the October war is particularly complex! Many of its possible results are contradictory.

It can generate more or less acceptable settlements, but it can also result in more conflicts during the coming years. Most Arabs have ambivalent feelings—one hand is prepared to reach out while the other is ready to close into a fist. Similarly, most Israelis probably waver between the temptation to restore the occupied territories and recognize the Palestinians in exchange for real coexistence with the Arabs and the temptation to prepare for a fifth war in order to return things to the way they were before 1973, when the Israelis felt so completely confident.

So that we find ourselves on very unstable psychological ground, where the aspirations of the people are contradictory, pulled both by the desire for peace and by the need for dignity and security. What is at stake, at this unusual moment in our history? Which aspects of the situation lead us in the direction of peace and which in the direction of another war?

We will often have occasion to return to this in detail. There are several possible peace settlements, depending on how deep we go in our search for solutions to the Arab-Israeli conflict. But the preliminary condition for even the most tentative peace settlement is the recognition by Israel of Egypt's and Syria's sovereign right over the occupied territories and the right of the Palestinian people to recognition of their existence as a nation.

These were the goals of the people who started the October war. And as long as these goals are not attained there will be other wars, because one hundred million Arabs consider these goals to be their inalienable, inevitable and entirely obvious rights.

My feeling is that many Israelis are well aware of this, and that they are now more or less prepared to agree. But unfortunately they have not found a new political leadership to replace the one that has been in power for the last fifty years, that of the first Zionist pioneers or the direct inheritors of their ideas.

This leadership has become an institution, an "establishment," with its own history, ideology, and inertia, and within the context of that institution, the Zionist ideal means the pursuit of Herzl's dream, the creation of a State of Israel extending out to its so-called historical frontiers, and the gradual gathering of all the Jews in the world within this state. The Israeli political leadership is nationalist in the narrowest sense of the term. For this leadership, the center of the world is the nation of Israel; the rest of the world consists of encouragements or obstacles to the flowering of that nation. From this point of view, the Arabs can only be obstacles.

Of course from the very beginning there have always been large differences of opinion within that leadership over the methods that should be employed, the alliances that should be formed, the tactics that should be used, the successive steps that should be taken in order to carry out the Zionist enterprise. We know that Weizmann and Ben-Gurion had two different attitudes toward alliance with Great Britain at the beginning of the Second World War, and we know that Ben-Gurion and Sharett had different ideas about the attempts at settlement with the Arabs immediately after the founding of the State of Israel.

No one can say what would have happened if the ones who had won out at each stage had been defeated instead. But what can be said is that each time circumstances favored the expansion of Jewish territory, before or after 1948, those who were in favor of expansion won out.

There is an almost natural, basic drive that carries Zionism toward expansion, since by definition every inch of Jewish territory has been taken from non-Jews—in this case, Arabs. Whether it was taken by force, trickery, or economic superiority, the fact remains the same—Israel is the natural product of continual expansion.

You say that the Israelis saw the war of 1967 as a defensive war; I don't believe it, but let's say it is true. When you found yourselves in possession of vast territories that you had never even dreamed of having before, what was the reaction that finally won out within the Zionist institution? Did you try to profit from this unique opporutnity to win over the Arabs by returning these territories in exchange for formal recognition of the State of Israel? Absolutely not.

Your reaction was to use the Sinai and the Golan Heights as buffer zones, but more importantly to acquire the Arab part of Jerusalem by annexing it in defiance of all the international agreements, and also to install yourselves solidly on the West Bank and end up by integrating it economically. These territories are part of "historic" Israel and most members of the Zionist establishment would certainly like to be able to keep them. The differences which arose over this matter did not challenge the profound conviction that these territories were part of the "historic patrimony of Israel," but bore on the problem of the one million Palestinians clinging to their land on the West Bank. The Israeli army was not able to drive them out, and they therefore created a terrible dilemma for the Zionists—we want this land, but we don't want these one million Arabs in our state.

The solution your leaders finally adopted was empirical, not codified—it confirmed that these territories belonged to historical Israel, it integrated them economically with official Israel, and it left the status of the Palestinian people in suspense. If that situation had lasted another six years, I belive that in one way or another it would have led to the permanent annexation of Palestine.

I don't think the basic political viewpoint of the Zionist establishment changed after 1973. What did change was the balance of forces in the region, the disposition of the populations. This is why the political tactics of the Israeli leaders necessarily had to change too. But for them it was a matter of adjusting to a situation that had suddenly become unfavorable, after six years during which they had more or less been able to lay down the law. And for this reason there were some forced retreats, some differences of opinion over how extensive these retreats should be, and some settling of personal accounts.

Did the new frame of mind, the new spirit that was appearing here and there, really extend to Israel? Did it move the Israelis to question the expansionist basis of Zionist ideology? It is possible that some leaders did question it, but very few; perhaps the new "doves" were among them, though I would not swear to it. But in any case, most of the important leaders, whether in the Likud or the Maarach—and in spite of the wide range of differences running all the way from the "hawks" in the Likud to the "doves" in the

Maarach—regard the Middle East in the same spirit as they did before.

They have not begun to understand the most important aspirations of the Arab people; they are no more aware now than they were before 1973 of the need to replace the old language with a new one, to speak of natural and inalienable rights instead of the balance of power and systems of security. They have not understood that a statement of principles on their part proclaiming recognition of Egypt's and Syria's right to the Sinai and the Golan Heights and the existence of Palestine as a nation is far more important for Israel's security in the long run than any international guarantees.

If they have not understood any of this, it has not been out of stupidity, but because for them the feelings of the Arab people simply do not count and because, in any case, they cannot benefit from recognizing Arab rights since this would permanently fix the borders of Israel within limits much narrower than those of historic Israel, and would completely prevent any possibility of future expansion. Their logic remains the same, though in a different context. They are temporizing, resisting each partial withdrawal as long as possible, while at the same time they continue to build up their arsenals, forcing the Arabs to follow suit.

If things go on this way, the large groups on both sides that are in favor of peace will become less and less audible, while the voices of the superpowers will become louder and louder because they are supplying the arms to both sides and backing them financially.

All this is taking us far away from the idea of peace.

Perhaps it is taking us towards a period of precarious, very unstable coexistence, which would be a result of the present overlapping of the interests of America and the Soviet Union, who are both looking for some kind of stabilization of the power relations established by the war of 1973. In the West there is a tendency to be glad that a dialogue has begun between the Arabs and the Israelis and to think that now everything else is secondary. Not at all.

The dialogue is beginning under terribly worrying conditions which could make it useless in the end. The negotiations at Geneva will not naturally and spontaneously lead to a reconciliation of the peoples involved. We must press hard if we want this to come about and if we want to find the real reasons for hope. The only real hope lies in the possibility—which is still very slim—of getting beyond this confrontation in its present form and giving the people a chance to deal with the huge domestic problems facing them, which will remain suspended as long as the conflict between the Arabs and the Israelis goes on.

Take Egypt's economic situation, for example. It is a disaster. The misery of most Egyptians is strikingly visible. Several million are out of work, most minor civil servants and industrial workers earn pitiful wages whose purchasing power has been cut in half over the last few years; the country people, who have emerged from their age-old submissiveness, can tolerate less and less the drain on their revenue by the cities for the support of industrialization, which is in a period of crisis.

The officials try to reassure everyone by implying that America will help us solve our economic problems. But how is America going to solve these problems? Has it ever transformed misery into prosperity in any Third World country? If it fulfills all its promises to rehabilitate the Suez Canal Zone, it might provide work over several years for a tiny fraction of the unemployed, which will be replaced by the growing population. Perhaps—but this is not at all certain—it will give new impetus to private enterprise and revitalize the market, which is to say that at best it will allow big business to prosper, and in its wake small business and part of the artisan class. And this would hurt the social security safety valves which Nasser instituted—particularly the policy of offering government work to everyone holding technical or advanced degrees.

This would mean the reversion to savage competition and rivalry that would get more and more out of control. Social harmony would not follow but rather a period of growing struggle among the classes.

So the crucial question that we ask ourselves is this: Will the Israelis allow the Arab masses to turn their efforts, their revolutionary energies, to the problems of democracy and economic well-being, by respecting once and for all their sovereign national rights? Or are they going to make the Arabs tighten their belts again for a long time to come in the attempt to regain these rights by war?

SAUL FRIEDLÄNDER: Once again, in your analysis of both the past and the present situation, your basic frame of reference is an explanation of Israeli attitudes and policies which for me does not correspond to reality at all. Once again, I could respond point by point to what for me is nothing but a series of mistaken opinions. I will refrain from doing this so that the debate can get out of this rut. But there is one aspect of things which I must try to explain to you as often and in as great detail as necessary, because I believe that a good many of our differences of opinion arise from it. As far as you can see, Israel's policy before and after 1973 was motivated by a desire to conquer and annex territory, a desire you think is deeply rooted in Zionism itself. For us, the Israelis, what seems to be a very slow movement in our policy is primarily the result of the most elementary caution, which has become more necessary than ever before, after the events of 1973.

Have you ever thought of the almost total isolation of Israel in October 1973, of the fact that nearly every nation—for reasons that were often sordid and coldly calculating—turned its back on a small country in danger? The hostility of the entire Communist world doesn't need to be described. And take the African nations—one after another, they cut all their ties with Israel, when it was Israel that had been suddenly attacked. As for Europe, you know where it stood. And I am not speaking only of France. As it happens, England was the most striking case. During the war the English put an embargo on weapons which were already on the docks, which Israel had paid for and was about to transport, and which the country most urgently needed. In the end Israel was left with only the Americans as allies—very powerful allies on whom we were almost entirely dependent and who could withdraw their support for any of various reasons if we did not comply with one or another of their demands.

So it is clear that the Israelis will be more flexible now about certain things than they were before 1973. But I will say, at the risk of being wrong, that they will be even more intractable than before about other things. The sense of how precarious their situation is and how isolated they are has increased during this last crisis, and they will demand minimum guarantees of survival all the more insistently because of that.

A while ago you said that after its victory in 1967 Israel could have made a generous gesture and created a set of conditions for the debate that would have made us more likely to reach an agreement. I don't know if that was possible. There were attempts, but they failed. But perhaps your general idea is right—it undoubtedly would have taken an even greater effort. Now it is up to the Arabs to try to put themselves in the Israelis' place and to show enough flexibility so that they don't force the Israelis into an impasse which could only result in another confrontation.

We have arrived at a unique point in this conflict, where both sides are ready to talk but are still seeing each other through distorting lenses. The balance is very unstable now, and I think it cannot last much longer. We will certainly be returning to the subject of the domestic struggles which make this balance delicate on both sides, but the description of the situation as we have heard it up to now is fairly revealing in itself. We find ourselves, therefore, faced with a unique opportunity, and we must seize it and make the most of it, or else there will be another war and everyone will lose by it in a very dramatic way.

The Negative Effect of the Great Powers

JEAN LACOUTURE: You gave two answers, Mahmoud Hussein, to the question "What changed for you in October 1973?" The first answer was: "We recovered our dignity as the conviction grew that we could now defend our independence as a nation." This is an important element. The second answer was: "Now the important problems—the social and economic problems, and the problem of democracy—are beginning to demand our attention again. We hope we will be able to settle our problems with Israel so that we can at last look after our own affairs." That is another important element. But aren't there other changes taking place for you?

MAHMOUD HUSSEIN: We really should emphasize the enormous effect of foreign involvement in the region on the future relations between Arabs and Israelis—the American involvement in particular.

The present situation, as I have said, and as I will often have to repeat, is very complex. Any brief account necessarily simplifies it, overemphasizes one or another of its aspects, especially since some of the most important aspects of it are not yet sufficiently clear. So we should try to define the negative aspects as well as the positive aspects of the changes that have come about since 1973.

On the positive side, the Arabs see the Israelis in a new spirit. To

define it in a few words, we can say that in the eyes of the Arabs,
Israel has once again taken on its true dimensions, those of a small
state which can still cause considerable trouble but is not really a
formidable danger. Between 1967 and 1973 it darkened the
horizon, it was The Enemy—the principal enemy, in Marxist
terminology. Even the United States seemed to be a distant enemy
by comparison and only to the extent that it supported Israel. You
may be astonished when I tell you that the sense of proportion of
many Arabs was so distorted that they had begun to see the United
States as the instrument of Israel and not the other way around. . .

After 1973 there was a saner, more realistic view. The people
who were most politically aware, in any case, tended more and
more to see American imperialism as the principal enemy;
established Zionism was merely one of its pawns, and it had many
others in the region, most in the very heart of the Arab world. As I
say, this was apparent only to the people who were most aware
politically, because to the others, who were influenced by the
official propaganda, the return in force of American influence
seemed in some way an Arab success. Washington had changed its
attitude, and after helping only Israel, had at last decided to
equalize the balance between Israel and the Arabs. In one sense this
was not entirely wrong, yet it was deceptive insofar as it implied
that the American change of heart was disinterested. It was not at
all disinterested. Washington was not detaching itself from Israel;
on the contrary, it was tying itself to Israel even more tightly than
before, but at the same time beginning to form connections with
certain Arab countries that up till then had been outside its sphere
of activities, like Egypt and perhaps Syria.

This rebalancing of American policy had the effect of anchoring
its influence more firmly in both camps. That is the important
negative aspect of the new situation. The United States is
reentering the Middle East with the great advantage of seeming to
many people to be a new friend.

SAUL FRIEDLÄNDER: Many things strike me about what Mahmoud
Hussein has just said. The first may not be very important, but I
hope you will excuse me if I speak of it, even emphasize it, since it
reinforces a point I made earlier this morning. You told us that

between 1967 and 1973 Israel had seemed to a number of Arabs to be a country which was not really dependent on the United States or any other Western country, but which in fact manipulated them to some degree.

By saying this you evoked a certain myth, the myth of all powerful Israel, I might say almost the myth of the Elders of Zion. We are talking about a notion borrowed directly from European anti-Semitism as I described it to you. I hope you won't mind my connecting these two things, but their connection is immediately obvious. You can see that it is easy to move from the European context, the anti-Semitic context, to the context of the Middle East. The Israelis are therefore not absolutely in the wrong when they consider that their present experience in the conflict with the Arab world is not entirely different from what has happened in the past. You Arabs yourselves—in specific circumstances, and perhaps without being very aware of it—are reviving certain myths which you have inherited directly from the most recent wave of European anti-Semitism, particularly the idea that the Jews are manipulating the world—which is pure madness.

JEAN LACOUTURE: I would like to point out, however, that there is a fundamental difference here between the Europeans and the Arabs. From the European point of view, Jewish control of world affairs (or European affairs) is pure fantasy, pure hallucination. It has no real basis. The fact that from time to time Jews have had important political roles in European countries—usually peaceful roles—is not enough to support this theory, which has always been imbecilic and became criminal in 1933.

The Arab point of view is different. For them, Israel's strength is a basic fact, like the ties between Israel and the United States. They cannot be accused of racism if they overestimated Israel's strength, if they believed that it had innumerable resources. More than anything, this was a way of justifying their weaknesses, their defeats...

MAHMOUD HUSSEIN: In this connection I must point out how much the Israeli leaders helped strengthen this illusion between 1967 and

1973. We should not forget that during the war of attrition, when there was a possibility that Moscow might send Soviet pilots over to join Egypt's air defenses, Dayan made a statement in which he asserted that Israel did not fear the Soviet Union, that Israel was strong enough to stand up against it... This was simply madness. Even the United States was worried about not being a match for the Soviet Union...

It is not surprising that when some of the less politically aware Arabs heard those words, they found their impression of a superimperialist Israel confirmed.

SAUL FRIEDLÄNDER: I don't remember that speech of Dayan's, but this isn't very important...

What I was trying to say is very simple: myths grow up quickly around Israel, and they cause the revival of certain fantasies that are part of European anti-Semitism. In the Middle East they are not necessarily charged with the same emotional violence that they carry among European anti-Semites. But all this reinforces a certain feeling on the part of the Israelis that there is a historical continuity, a continuity in their isolation and the tendency for other people to surround the country, the group, the community, with myths that have no basis in reality—that, in short, people refuse to accept Israel as a group of human beings like other human beings, with their good and their bad sides. For this reason—and here I come to the second part of what you said—it is very encouraging to hear that in your eyes and in the eyes of the Arabs whose feelings you express here, Israel has taken on its human proportions again. You added that Israel is a Middle Eastern country like the others, confronted with somewhat the same problems.

I must emphasize that I do not agree with your Marxist analysis of the situation in general and the situation in the Middle East in particular. I have a different point of view, and if I had to define my position politically, I could say that I am a liberal rather than a socialist. This does not matter very much at this point in the debate, but might perhaps become more important when we examine the prospects for the future. I do not necessarily, therefore, share your revolutionary concepts; but I am absolutely in agreement when you recognize that Israel is a country like other countries in the Middle East, a small country among others, and like the others, often manipulated by the great powers.

What you said leads naturally to an idea that many Israelis have expressed in the course of the last few years, namely that there can be no *true* peace until the people of the region come to an agreement together without the mediation of a third power. You must admit that for a long time the Israelis have wanted to engage in a *direct* dialogue without the intervention of the United Nations or the Americans or the Russians, having come to understand, I suppose—even though I admit they may have had some ulterior motives—that only on that level would the countries of the area be able to come to an agreement, and that the intervention of a great power would only complicate the situation to the latter's profit and confuse the issue.

You have expressed an idea in which I believe very deeply. After the first "helping hand" from the Americans and the Russians, which is no doubt necessary, we must manage to come to an understanding among ourselves. It may not be possible on a political level, but it is certainly possible within the context of private discussion groups whose duty it would be to clarify the problems and devise plans for the future, and where Arabs and Israelis would have to talk things over without the mediation of any third party—by which I mean representatives of the great powers and of other interests. You have expressed an important idea, and I subscribe to it completely. It will be between Arabs and Israelis that contact is made.

JEAN LACOUTURE: Saul Friedländer's remarks have conveniently taken us from the historical "leap" of 1967 to the even more decisive one of 1973. We all agree that the war which one side calls the Yom Kippur War and the other the Ramadan War, and which we will simply call the war of October 1973, in some way has brought us here together. That is why I would like to ask Mahmoud Hussein two questions.

One consequence of that war which was important to the whole world was that it made Israel seem vulnerable. People in Israel probably thought, as people did elsewhere, that the next time, or another time, Israel might be beaten. However—and I would like to ask Mahmoud Hussein why this was—we practically never heard the Arabs saying this sort of thing: "This time we have them, the next time it will be for good. It isn't worth our while to talk to them because we're going to beat them. Let's go on the way we're going, and we'll win in October 1975 or October 1978..." I'm well aware that cynicism like this is relatively rare, but it did exist here and there in the Arab world, and not only due to Shukairy. Cries of death to Israel have been heard fairly often; it might have been only natural to hear them at the moment Israel became historically vulnerable, confronting an Arab coalition whose strength was growing. Why do you think these cries were not heard?

My second question is this. When did you say to yourself, Mahmoud Hussein, "Now I am ready to talk to an Israeli"? When did this happen? You found this idea inconceivable during the summer of 1973. Why, how, and at what moment did you realize that dialogue had become possible, and even useful to you as a militant Arab leftist?

MAHMOUD HUSSEIN: Before answering you, I would like to make one remark about the direct dialogue which the Israelis have been suggesting to the Arabs for so long.

I do not want to disappoint Friedländer, but I think that a direct dialogue before 1973 would have had a fundamentally different meaning from what it has today. Before 1973 Israel was in a powerful position, and there were no truly representative political sectors in Israel prepared to talk to us in a serious way about the essential needs of Arab sovereignty.

You ask me, Jean Lacouture, why dialogue is possible now. Well, because I think part of Israel is now capable of understanding the vital importance regaining sovereignty over their territories has for the Egyptian and Syrian peoples, and the similar importance being recognized as a nation has for the Palestinians. And because I think Israel could do something about this if it realizes that Arab recognition of the Israeli community would result from it.

So, our discussion might become the first contact between the

Arabs and the Israelis; that is why attempting it is worthwhile. When did we realize that this contact was possible? Our answer can be dated—it made a great stir at the time. It was a letter published by *Le Nouvel Observateur* on 22 October 1973—in the middle of the war.

Once the Arabs' pride had been restored, the peoples of the region had better things to do than continue killing each other off for the benefit of the great powers. From then on there existed the possibility, however slight, of joining together in order to liberate their land from the interference of the great powers.

For this, it is true, there would have to be an immense upset in the way Israelis were accustomed to seeing things, since you had always turned to the West for support in your fight against us. Now you would have to begin to rely on us and join us in fighting the West. And it is the more difficult for you to the extent that Western aid has performed a fundamentally different function for you than it has for us.

For us this aid was deceptive because it really took back more than it gave and was a disguised form of exploitation that weakened and diminished us; while for you it has always come as a surplus, increasing your economic and military capacity and allowing you to live well above your means. Until now, therefore, there has been a solidarity between you and the imperialist West which is understandable, since even if there were many of you who weren't aware of it, you were actually guarding the imperialist West against the Arab national movement.

Now all that must change. Is it possible, or is it only a dream? It will be up to you to say. I can only hope that in spite of the material advantages you have drawn from your integration with the West, most of you will place above everything else the desire to feel at home, at last, in the Middle East, and that to bring that about you will be able to break the umbilical cord which until now has tied you to our enemies.

In conclusion I would like to say that in my own position there has been both continuity and development since 1973. Until the war I was one of the people who joined the progressive Palestinians in trying to work out a future which would provide a place for the Israeli community.

The goal of destroying the apparatus of the Israeli state, which was the strategic resolution of this group, never meant what people in Israel so often thought it meant. It never meant the destruction of the population of the State of Israel, but only the dissolution of its racist, anti-Arab structure.

The idea of a democratic state which would replace the Jewish state with a multinational or multidenominational state left a place open for the Jewish community while answering the deepest primary need—to dissociate that community from the Zionist war machine. What needs to be reexamined in this formulation is not its theoretical goal, which is, abstractly speaking, irreproachable, but the conception it contains of the stages which should lead to a fertile reconciliation between Palestinians and Israelis.

Until 1973 it seemed to us that the process of a sustained popular war would gradually bring the Arab masses and the Israeli masses to the point of challenging the system of imperialist domination which was enclosing the Middle East, a system of which the Zionist institution was not the only support, but the most solid. The Israeli state apparatus had to be destroyed, therefore, just as did the apparatus of some of the Arab states insofar as these structures were tied to the system of domination.

From this point of view, the meeting between the Arabs and the Israelis would take place on the very battleground of the fight for liberation, and the problems of their relations within a liberated Palestine would not be specifically posed.

Today this plan is out of date, because the war of October gave back to the principal Arab states enough political initiative to permit them to engage in dialogue with Israel, and because from then on the Arab masses began to turn their hopes in another direction—the struggle for the internal transformation of their society. The contradictions, as they were seen at the popular level, became different, and therefore the priorities for the fight also became different. This being the case, the forces of change and renewal in the Arab world will not have to assert themselves and organize themselves within the framework of a popular war against Israel, but within the framework of mass movements against the conservative ruling classes.

This is a basic element in the new situation, but that does not mean that the imperialist domination will be forgotten. The class contradictions in the heart of the Arab world lead to a fight against political and economic supervision by the great powers. In their relations with the Arabs, the Israelis are therefore called upon, now more than ever before, to choose which side they want to be on. This choice, which would have faced the Israelis in the course of a popular war before 1973, will now face them within the framework of the State of Israel itself; but they will not be able to avoid the choice, for it will determine whether or not Israel enters into the community of the people of the region.

SAUL FRIEDLÄNDER: Unfortunately, at the end of this first day of dialogue, Mahmoud Hussein's last remarks are very disquieting: "Zionist war machine," the "irreproachable theoretical goal" of the formulation for a "multinational state" in Palestine, and so forth. Of course, Mahmoud Hussein's very last words seemed to express a more moderate position, but that does not make his preceding formulations any less explicit. I don't know if he realizes what these formulations mean to us. I must ask him to consider carefully whether these definitions are the only ones he can conceive of in all honesty. Of course, if they do seem the only possible ones to him, he will say so and we will know where we stand. He clearly has the right to want to break the Arab state apparatus. That is his business. He is an Arab and he can judge the affairs of the Arab world. He can even hope—and here I'm going quite far—that one day the "Zionist State," as he calls it, will wither away. But if he poses as a condition for settlement between the Arabs and the Israelis the destruction of the State of Israel in favor of a democratic Palestine or—it hardly matters—a multinational democratic state, in other words, the Palestinian formula, I can assure him right now that no Israeli, not a single one, will accept this formula—not even the Communist members of the Rakah. He should know in advance that even if he believes this formulation is the only precondition for a settlement, what it means is no settlement at all. Israel must remain a sovereign state, master of its own destiny, a Zionist state—I say it plainly and I will explain what it means later on—and this is obviously the absolute precondition to any solution.

I must say to Mahmoud Hussein, you should think carefully before you revert to that formula, you should realize where it is leading us. It will not stop the debate, because we want to cover all the questions—but if you go on talking in these terms, we will come to a total impasse.

MAHMOUD HUSSEIN: There is certainly a difference, a fundamental difference, between us concerning the development of the situation in the long run. We have two different strategic visions of the socio-economic contradictions which determine that development, and of their possible solutions. But that is in the long run. We will explore it in depth in the course of the third day. Now we must examine the problems of the immediate future.

II

Second Day: The Present

Real Forces of Change

JEAN LACOUTURE: During the first day of our talks, we examined the past, which gave us a chance to describe the elements in the Arab-Israeli conflict that were impeding the process of change. We agreed that after the ambiguous disruptions of 1967, the war of October 1973 allowed us to cross a historic dividing line, and that from then on almost everything was different.

Up to this point we have essentially kept to psychological, rather subjective ground; now we would like to describe the objective factors of change, the new phase in history that began with the war of October 1973, and deal with it from the point of view of what the facts were, what really happened, what the objective situation was. To begin with, we will hear from Friedländer.

SAUL FRIEDLÄNDER: As far as Israel is concerned, I don't think your way of formulating things is quite right. In my opinion there has been no radical change in Israel's concrete, objective position since 1973. Certain factors which were already manifest or latent before have grown stronger. We can look at the facts of Israel's situation on several levels: Israel and the great powers, Israel and the Arabs, and Israel's internal evolution. We have to ask what changed on each level and what did not change.

73

I think the word that would best sum up the situation on the first two levels would be the term "asymmetry." I will try to explain what I mean by it.

In this debate I do not have to remind you of one thing that is absolutely clear—that all of the great powers have major strategic and economic interests in the Middle East because of its geographic position and its natural resources. The great powers enter the region one after another as rivals—first the French and the English, then the Americans who try to supplant the first two and succeed, and finally the Americans and the Soviets in a confrontation which began in the fifties and is still going on now, in a form that is not really different from what it was then.

Why is there "asymmetry," from Israel's point of view? Because the Arabs have almost everything to offer the great powers while Israel has very few assets. First of all, the Arabs have space—and therefore control of the strategic routes—and access to the region's great seaports; they are in a position to give or refuse important bases to any of the powers. They control the mineral resources, and we know how important they are. There is no point in going into the details, which every reader is familiar with and which we obviously know well, but as an example let us consider things from the Soviet point of view. By establishing itself more or less openly in the Arab countries of the Machrek or in Egypt, the USSR can accomplish five or six things at the same time. It can circumvent NATO's system of defense, as has been frequently pointed out; it can penetrate into black Africa; it can move toward the Persian Gulf and then into the Indian Ocean—which is essential not only because of the conflict with the United States but also because of the conflict with China; and it can put its hands on the essential resources of the area, not only in its own interest but also, more importantly, to prevent these resources from being controlled by anyone else.

For the Americans, the problem is just the opposite. They have to stop the Russians from penetrating into the region. There are also direct advantages for them, of course, particularly in control of the oil.

The Arabs have almost everything to give, almost everything to offer or refuse. There was a time when people could take anything they wanted from the Arabs by force. Today that is no longer possible. As things are now, it is not easy to occupy Saudi Arabia and take control of its oil; the Americans are not thinking of landing military forces in Saudi Arabia in order to force it to give up its oil.

JEAN LACOUTURE: And yet the Pentagon did consider occupying Abu Dhabi during the crisis of October 1973. It seems that American strategists did not rule out the idea of a "quick strike" operation against one or another Arab oil producer if it was recalcitrant and at the same time not protected by the USSR.

MAHMOUD HUSSEIN: It should be made clear that before 1973 certain American politicians publicly advocated this idea. What was in question was not the occupation of a few small islands in the gulf, but of all the oil-bearing regions in Saudi Arabia, at the time when King Faisal was beginning to consider reducing oil production. At that time, this act of basic national sovereignty seemed unthinkable to the Americans. We should add that certain Israelis in positions of responsibility added fuel to the fire by suggesting that Israeli commandos be the ones to carry out this operation.

SAUL FRIEDLÄNDER: I don't know what American thinking on this subject was, but as far as the occupation of Saudi Arabia by Israel is concerned, I don't see how...

In the long run, anyway, this is an unthinkable situation. So I would like to return to my first idea: the Arab world can give or refuse to give whatever it likes—it is holding extraordinarily good cards. Within the bargaining situation as a whole, it is in a strong position, and Israel is in a very weak one. This is therefore the first asymmetry. Israel facing the great powers has very few things to give. There may be a small Israeli market for some American or Western exporters, but that does not amount to much. The mineral resources of Israel are mostly sand with a few stones mixed in. As for bases, Israel might offer the use of some of them, and that is a potential asset. But on the whole, there is an obvious asymmetry.

JEAN LACOUTURE: I would like to raise another objection. The Israeli army is nevertheless an important factor in the Middle East. I don't agree with this theory myself, but an American strategist would think that the Israeli army, combined with the armies of Turkey and Iran, forms a very considerable counterbalance not only in the relations between the Israelis and the Arabs but in a larger Western strategy in the Middle East. Considering the anti-Arab feelings prevalent in Ankara and Teheran, the uniting of these forces—the Iranian, Turkish and Israeli—which are the three best armies in the Middle East at present, is an objective which at least some American groups have not abandoned.

SAUL FRIEDLÄNDER: I don't agree. It is certainly true that the Israeli army represents a very real force, and I believe that to a certain extent even the Russians must take it into account. But I can't see the United States organizing a coordinated Turkish, Iranian, and Israeli force. This plan dates back to the fifties and no longer means anything. The Turks and the Iranians would never ally themselves with Israel in any undertaking that was not strictly secret. Turkey and Iran are still Moslem countries and have predominantly Moslem sympathies; they would not want to cut themselves off from the Arab world. Israel is a force acting for itself, period.

But what I want to bring out is the disparity between the Israeli position and the Arab position in relation to the great powers, the disparity between what each of them can give the great powers or take away from them. This fundamental asymmetry was increased by the October war.

For one thing, the war of 1973 saw the emergence of oil as a weapon—and I think it was shown to be more powerful than even the Arabs had imagined, more powerful than anyone had imagined. Up to that point, oil had been a hypothetical weapon. Now it had become a real weapon, even though it was only used in a very marginal way during the 1973 crisis. Its magical effect is undeniable. But I think this effect is produced by the fear of oil as a weapon rather than by any actual use of it. The Japanese, the Europeans, the Africans, the whole world turned its back on Israel, and even the Americans found themselves in an embarrassing situation. In the end, Israel was left alone with the United States, which in turn meant that it would find itself in an extremely difficult position if it happened that Israel's vital interests were to diverge from America's plans. I will say more about this in a moment. So you can see that the asymmetry between the Israelis and the Arabs in relation to the major powers became only more pronounced during the 1973 crisis, and it is a situation that we cannot forget.

This puts Israel is a difficult position, which could be described as one of extreme dependence on the United States, both economically and militarily, and Israel is forced to take this dependence into account in each major decision that is made. For Israel to cut itself off from the Americans and stand alone, or even adopt policies contrary to Washington's express will, would create enormous problems. Yet, suppose the Americans demand something which seems reasonable to them but which does not seem either reasonable or viable to Israel—something which actually threatens what Israel considers to be a vital interest. It seems to me that Israel could be faced with this dilemma in the coming months and years, because of its situation in relation to the major powers. To give you a concrete example, suppose the Americans say: Sharm-el-Sheikh is not essential to Israel, Israel can afford to give back all of the Sinai Desert to Egypt, including Sharm-el-Sheikh; there is nothing to worry about, we guarantee protection of the straits. Suppose—I don't say this is the case, but it's not completely impossible—the Israelis decide that it is essential to maintain their presence in Sharm-el-Sheikh, that without it the whole security of Israel would be endangered. This is an argument that can be made, that has already been made several times. It would present the possibility of an American-Israeli confrontation. Even further, suppose the Egyptians say: "We will not sign a peace treaty until Sharm-el-Sheikh is restored to us," and the Americans side with Egypt. That could very well happen.

What would Israel do in this sort of dilemma, being so extremely dependent on the Americans? I am trying to show the problem involved in the asymmetry in relation to the major powers, and this is going to lead me to draw certain conclusions.

The second asymmetry is in relation to the Arabs. It has always existed. At this point I will not go back over facts which I've already covered, except to say that a situation in which three million Israelis are forced to confront more than a hundred million Arabs, backed by a Moslem community which is admittedly not unified but which numbers hundreds of millions of people and which in turn has the support of the rest of the Third World, and so on, and so forth—is a clear example of a fundamental asymmetry. I therefore believe, as I said before, that the Yom Kippur War only clarified a situation which had been obvious to any perceptive observer long before and which had been somewhat obscured by what had been going on before then.

The war of 1973 did not suddenly mark the growth of unlimited Arab power or the inexorable decline of Israel. Not at all. What we're concerned with are long-term tendencies which were evident before, during, and after the war. Arab strength is increasing, slowly or not so slowly; Israel's strength is also growing—not declining—but the two curves could eventually meet. The gap is not widening in Israel's favor; in the very long run it is widening in the Arabs' favor. I think time is not on Israel's side in this conflict.

Which leads me to conclude that Israel must consider every possibility for negotiation. But again, what should we do if our antagonist's demands challenge the very survival of the state? We find ourselves faced with a second dilemma directly tied to the first. One can imagine the Arabs saying: "We'll negotiate, but there must be an absolute, unconditional, and immediate return to the borders of 1967." A demand like that would be considered by most Israelis as an imminent and mortal danger. Or imagine the following Arab declaration: "We want to deal fairly with you, providing you abandon your Zionist aspirations." This precondition seems even less acceptable to me than all the others, because it challenges the very essence of Israel—as a place of return, a home for any Jew who wants to settle there. This is the dilemma: I think we must negotiate, but what would happen if, during the negotiations, we were denied what we consider to be the most rudimentary bases for our survival? Israel would naturally build a sort of fortress and shut itself up in it to wait and see, but obviously that would be a dismal prospect.

You might ask, "How does all this influence domestic policy?" And that brings me to my last point.

I have already described the ways of thinking in Israel about the fate of the occupied territories and the possibilities for settlement. I have explained in particular the position of the governmental majority, what one could call the group in favor of reasonable compromise.

What were the consequences of the October war on this level? It increased awareness of the urgent need for negotiation and at the same time increased awareness of the need to safeguard the essential guarantees of security—seeing that both the beginning and the subsequent course of the hostilities had shown up a vulnerability in Israel which was perhaps obvious to some, but which since 1967 had not been obvious to everyone. Therefore, on the one hand, absolute necessity for dialogue and compromise, but on the other, greater care not to sell off what was essential and vital, since 1973 had demonstrated that the balance of power was not changing to the advantage of Israel. We are therefore confronted by a series of dilemmas, almost a series of possible impasses, and faced with very difficult problems whose solutions will almost certainly have to be found within the coming months and no later.

JEAN LACOUTURE: Couldn't we add one rather significant nuance to your picture, relating to what we could call the central current of opinion? The 1973 conflict seems to have accentuated the differences between the "doves" of the establishment and the group in power. The current led by Arieh Eliav and Ben-Aharon, for example, is more clearly marked by a pacifist tendency than is the central group. Couldn't we speak of a group which does not display as much boldness as the militants of the extreme left who are challenging Zionism or who are partisans of peace at any price, but which is perhaps the core of a peace party, more determined than the leadership of the Labor Party?

SAUL FRIEDLÄNDER: Yes, you are quite right to emphasize that. In fact, I think that Eliav and Ben-Aharon represent a group that is in the very heart of the Labor Party yet is in favor of bolder compromise than is the official leadership of the party.* But I think that in the end it is a matter of nuances rather than fundamental differences, except on one point—and even on this point, now, the official position is full of nuances—namely, the question of the Palestinians. For Eliav and Ben-Aharon, as for me, there is no doubt about the existence of a Palestinian people, and in negotiations this must be taken into account from the very beginning. There can be arguments within Israel itself about which tactic to follow, but Eliav, Ben-Aharon and perhaps even some Labor ministers of the present government do not think there is any question about recognition as such of the existence of the Palestinians as a people. But for many other members of the Labor Party, perhaps even the majority, this point provokes hesitation and reluctance, possibly even refusal. There must therefore be a distinction.

As far as the frontiers go, perhaps the small minority you refer to would be ready for even larger compromises than the majority, but when we come to specific details, we will see that there is no great difference between Eliav and Rabin, whereas between Eliav and Dayan there is a considerable difference. Dayan is quite close to the Likud, because of his pessimistic view of things.

MAHMOUD HUSSEIN: There are many points in your account that I would like to bring up again in the course of the discussion because they should be explored in depth. For example, the impossibility of Israel's giving up the law of return. To use the metaphor you used yesterday, this is another bomb in the midst of the dialogue. But we will see later whether it can be dismantled or whether it has to go off.

Within the context of the topics decided on for today we should limit ourselves to analyzing the objective facts, the balance of forces which emerged from the October war. I want to begin by saying that I think there were profound changes, not only in the Arab world but in Israel too. Between 1967 and 1973 there was certainly dissymmetry between the two sides, but it worked to

---

*Since this was said, Arieh Eliav has left the Labor Party; he is now an independent member of the Israeli Parliament.

Israel's advantage. The assets which you attribute to the Arabs were only potential assets. Actually, the active dissymmetry, the one that impressed itself on the area and on the minds of the people was that of an unyielding state, relying on an omnipotent army, intervening wherever it wanted to, whenever it wanted to, as against states that were disunified and becoming weaker. The dissymmetry that exists now is obviously not the same as the dissymmetry that existed before 1973, but things are much less simple than you make them out to be.

Of course the Arabs have numbers, space, and mineral resources on their side, and I am tempted to say that this is only natural; they are the sons of this land and they have a right to everything it contains and everything they have created here. But so far, and for a long time to come, this is only potential possession. You say, "They can give or refuse to give whatever they like." But they would still have to be really free to give or refuse, meaning they would have to have effective control over their fate and their wealth. You speak as though the Arabs were already free of all foreign supervision—which is not the case.

Besides, Israel is not there as an impartial spectator, it is not simply a witness to the imperialist presence, but plays a constant, more or less effective role in the consolidation of this presence, in the weakening of the Arabs' desires for national liberation. Within the framework of the Zionist vision, Israel has bet on the side of the imperialist presence and against Arab independence. So that if we look at things as they really are now, we see that the principal asymmetry is actually still working to the advantage of the opponents of independence, and against the ability of the Arabs to keep control of their space and their wealth.

It is not a situation of Israel being on one side, alone and poor, and a united Arab front on the other side, sovereign and rich, and the great powers posed between them, wondering which side to be on. These great powers have been here for a long time. The United States is well anchored in the area, leaning on solid structures like the armies of Israel, Iran or Turkey, and also on structures that are not as solid, like the ruling classes in Saudi Arabia, Jordon and Lebanon. At the moment it is trying to induce Egypt and Syria to join it.

Friedländer has just rejected the idea of a coalition among Israel,

Iran, and Turkey which would occupy the Arab world for the benefit of the United States. But the Arab world can be dominated without being occupied, and the armies of the three countries in question can take part in this domination simply because their presence represents a constant threat. They do not need to coordinate their action directly in order to achieve this. To take only one recent example, Iran and Israel certainly exerted similar and complementary pressure on Saudi Arabia in the interests of the United States when Riyadh proposed a modification of its oil strategy.

> JEAN LACOUTURE: We could also cite the very obvious example of Iran's pressure on Iraq during the October war. The revival of the Kurd troubles, which Iran had something to do with, froze the Iraqi force (insofar as it would have come out to fight), and this formed part of Israel's objective support in the crisis.

MAHMOUD HUSSEIN: All this tends to show that the image of asymmetry cannot be applied as you have applied it, Friedländer, to the situation as it really is now. And you can't ask the Arabs to remain militarily weaker than Israel in order to compensate for Israel's small number of people...

SAUL FRIEDLÄNDER: Just one remark to make my thinking absolutely clear. There is no question in my mind of making the Arabs compensate for Israel's geographical or natural deficiencies, if one can use that word. Israel must negotiate a settlement with the Arabs under conditions and with provisions that do not challenge its very survival. The question is not one at all of demanding vast territories or the annexation of whole populations, but in fact small areas, really tiny from the Arabs' point of view while they may be essential for Israel, at least temporarily.

MAHMOUD HUSSEIN: All right. Now what can we say about the new balance of forces that was established in October 1973? I think it can be summed up as two series of changes. For one thing, there was an increase in the direct influence of the superpowers on the course of events; for another, the Arab states grew stronger in relation to Israel. We do not want to say, as some say rather unthinkingly, that the superpowers can do whatever they like. First of all, they are in conflict with each other, which leaves the opposing forces of the region a certain margin for maneuvering. Then, these powers are obliged to take into account certain irrepressible aspirations of the people, and also the particular interests of the leading local forces, whose support was essential to them for establishing their influence in the region.

But be this as it may, Washington and Moscow are the ones who have control over the flow of arms and the massive economic credits—not to mention their fleets, which are patrolling all around us. The solutions that are proposed at each stage of the Arab-Israeli negotiations will have to pass through these two capitals, or at least one of them, before they can be translated into action. Nothing can diverge from a framework which both superpowers would find acceptable.

And what do they want? Though they may be in competition with one another, I think they feel the same way about not wanting to give up control of the area. They apparently want to ensure that there is a rather flexible status quo, one which can adjust to changes, but in which the dangers of confrontation can be avoided as far as possible without either of the two opposing camps gaining clear ascendancy over the other. This sort of situation provides the firmest foundation for their presence in the Middle East; what is important for them is that both sides remain dissatisfied, continue to mistrust one another and feel the need of the protection of a great power.

The Arab protagonists are playing the game. You might even say that the Arab governments that prepared the October 1973 war were trying to arrive at this point—of convincing the great powers that things could not go on as they had since 1967, and that they should intervene so this indirect dialogue could take place, this protected dialogue that the Arabs had been praying for.

Yet as they enter into discussion with Israel, their word carries more weight because of the very fact that they started the October war and came out of it undefeated.

Before they started the war they did everything possible to avoid it. In the opinion of the Arab people, their governments neither could nor would want to take the risk of engaging in another confrontation. Everyone remembered how the war of attrition had ended, when Nasser had originally wanted to confine it to the area of the canal. The Israeli government had ordered the bombing of Egyptian cities then, and Golda Meir had declared that she intended to induce the people to revolt, hoping that this would force Nasser to abandon his attempts to change the situation by force. The war ended only when the Russians agreed to protect the canal and the large cities with a network of SAM's. This did not inspire great confidence in the power of the Arab armies.

Then what led the governments of Egypt and Syria, backed by Saudi Arabia and Algeria in particular, to make serious preparations for the October offensive? Well, it was the feeling that their regimes were threatened; that their political credibility, their authority over their people, had been deeply affected. Israel's supremacy, and its arrogance on top of that, were a provocation to the Arabs that was all the more intolerable because of the fact that Iran was taking advantage of this state of affairs to agitate in certain Arab states and heighten even further the general feeling of humiliation—whether by using the Kurd question as an excuse to intervene in Iraq or by seizing the three small Arab islands in the gulf.

One by one, all the Arab leaders were beginning to feel vulnerable. Israel and Iran were becoming the true regional powers, and the United States was apparently counting on the fact that this would lead the nationalist Arab regimes to break all their ties with the USSR little by little or fall apart. No doubt it was this brutal provocation which finally brought about Egypt's and Syria's decision to prepare the October 6th offensive and which led to the almost complete unity of the Arabs around Presidents Sadat and Assad.* These leaders were taking a gamble. They staked everything they had and they won the bet, in the sense that they achieved the exact goal they had fixed for themselves: to force the superpowers to intervene and begin a process of negotiation that

---

*Hafez Assad, a Syrian general and leader of the "moderate" wing of Ba'ath, a socialist and pan-Arab party; he became head of the Damascus government in 1971.

would not be dishonorable for the Arabs, and which would even obtain the support of their peoples.

Because of this, they acquired a dependable capacity for political initiative after the month of October, and as a consequence a new bargaining power in relation to Israel.

SAUL FRIEDLÄNDER: Mahmoud Hussein, in passing you mentioned the Israeli policy of intensive bombing of Egypt during the war of attrition in 1970. You explained this policy by describing an Israeli analysis of the Egyptian situation which comes close, in some ways, to my own analysis.

I must say right away that I was against the intensive bombing and as soon as it began I wrote an article that appeared in *Maariv* (an Israeli evening paper) saying that it was a serious mistake and would lead the Russians to send pilots and take direct responsibility for the protection of the canal zone and the interior of Egypt. So that I am only reiterating my own position on this point. But it is important to outline what the official reasoning was at that time. The same asymmetry keeps recurring, and the same general idea: Israel cannot allow several of its young people to be killed every day on the banks of the Suez Canal, and must therefore prevent the daily artillery fire that inflicts this kind of loss, which is intolerable both objectively and psychologically. What is more, every day at that time, the Israeli newpapers published photographs of the men who had just been killed on the Suez Canal—a very humane way to honor the fallen soldiers, perhaps, but its psychological effect was undeniably a feeling of perpetual mourning. This may seem strange to you, Mahmoud Hussein, since you come from a country of more than thirty million people and to you, Jean Lacouture, since you live in a country of fifty-five million. You will say, "In the long run, what do a few deaths matter?" Once again this is Israel's particular situation, where everyone knows everyone else. (One doesn't really know each soldier who is killed along the whole of the Suez, but the country is so small that if you put the soldier's name and where he comes from under his photograph, a great many people may know, or think they know, his family.) The result is that in some way the grief of each family is widely shared, and this would have become unbearable very quickly. So it "had to change" at any price, and this explains the intensive bombing. It was an attempt to disorganize completely the Egyptian artillery concentrations and lines of supply, and put an end to the war of attrition that Nasser had begun.

MAHMOUD HUSSEIN: I mentioned only one element of Golda Meir's analysis during the war of attrition. I said only that Israel's leaders recognized the fear that the development of a mass movement was causing Nasser, and that there was therefore a sort of complicity between Israel's leaders and Nasser in the face of the possibility of a similar development. But instead of inducing Golda Meir to offer a formula for compromise, this only increased her intransigence. Here I am simply pointing out the gap between the Israeli leaders and the most moderate of the Arab leaders before 1973.

Now I would like to say something about the respect with which you treat the dead. If we disregard the context in which your wars take place, this attitude deserves to be admired, whether it is present in a large country or a small one. Man as a human being has not yet acquired that degree of importance for us. I was very shocked to see on television that when prisoners of the October war were exchanged and Golda Meir and Moshe Dayan went to the airport to greet the Israeli prisoners, Sadat did not even dream of going anywhere to welcome the Egyptian prisoners. What was even worse was that the authorities did not allow the people to show them the affection they had every right to expect. It is possible that the status of the Egyptian soldier has improved a little in the eyes of the authorities over what it was before 1967, but it still does not amount to much.

SAUL FRIEDLÄNDER: Your last remarks, I think, are far more important than the discussion would make them seem at first, because you are recognizing an aspect of Israel that is rather moving, and you also see that there are some things that are not yet the way they should be, particularly in Egyptian society. I don't mean to be sentimental, but sometimes it is hard not to emphasize the emotional aspect of certain situations. I believe that it is essential to the dialogue that both sides acknowledge the constant human misery and human sacrifice inherent in this conflict.

Besides this, there are two points in your remarks that Jean Lacouture has called attention to: I feel I must respond to them.

If I have understood you correctly, you see Israel as an objective instrument of American policy in the Middle East; for you, it was such an instrument even before 1973, it's still more of one now—like Iran, for example—even if subjectively the Israelis do not see things in this light.

MAHMOUD HUSSEIN: One small correction. I purposely did not use the term ''instrument.'' These days, there are hardly any countries left that are simply instruments in the hands of a great power. Rather, I stressed the fact that the extent of Israel's dependence on the United States varied according to the circumstances, that between 1967 and 1973 Israel acquired a clear autonomy of decision, an autonomy which it lost somewhat during the October war. So that there is a relationship of alliance, or rather patronage, whose terms have not been definitely set forth.

SAUL FRIEDLÄNDER: Whatever Israel's objective dependence may be, arising from its relative weakness compared to a great power—in this case, the United States—Israel has such a deeply rooted sense of what is peculiarly Israeli, and of its will to remain what it is, that there are obvious limits to this dependence. It is perfectly clear, for example, that if the Americans demanded a change in the conception of the very nature of Israel—meaning an end to immigration, to ''Zionism''—the refusal would be immediate, absolute and irrevocable. Israel feels itself to be a special community—and it is reproached for feeling this—a distinctive entity which in addition is accustomed to being in some way pressed flat between the great powers. The present situation is perhaps especially dramatic. Nevertheless, Israel does not want to be in any way an extension of the United States, a country which would be forced to follow American policy. Israel is afraid of a confrontation with the Americans, but it will certainly come to that if the Americans go beyond certain limits in what they demand.

JEAN LACOUTURE: I would like to ask you to describe an example (I know there are some) of opposition, or strong contradiction, between the Israeli government and the American government. You alluded to this apropos of Sharam-el-Sheikh. Could we go back to that? Can you tell us how this contradiction worked at one time in connection with the Rogers Plan, in connection with Resolution 242,* when Gahal left the government? Do you honestly think there was a risk of a crisis occurring in relations between Israel and the United States?

SAUL FRIEDLÄNDER: As soon as you started to ask your question, of course, I thought of the Rogers Plan. The first Rogers Plan, of 1969. When the Americans proposed this plan, the Israeli government realized that it involved evacuating almost all the occupied territories without any reciprocal concessions, in other words, without the guarantees of security that it was constantly demanding. You doubtless remember that Rogers asked Israel to return to the old frontiers with some slight modifications; this was completely inadequate from Israel's point of view. The answer came immediately—within a few days, if I remember correctly. It was an absolute and categorical "no." Nothing much happened then, but you may ask what would happen if there actually were a break between the United States and Israel. I spoke of this possibility a while ago without answering the question. It goes without saying that there is no obvious answer, but we can try to see it a little more clearly by asking another hypothetical question: What would have happened in 1938 if Beneš had said no to the Munich "Diktat"?

I have often wondered what would have happened if, faced with the "Diktat" imposed by the great powers, Beneš had said: "We don't accept this, we intend to fight." I think that if this had happened the Czechs' will to resist would have obliged the others, goaded by public opinion, to side with the Czechs and enter the fray in some manner or other. I realize that this hypothetical example, transposed to Israel, contradicts our own past experience

*A UN resolution adopted on 22 November 1967 in New York. The text calls for the actual recognition by the Arabs of the State of Israel and Israel's evacuation of the territories occupied in June 1967 (according to the French text) or simply "territories" (according to the English text).

and even certain other recent cases. Yet there is still reason to
believe that faced with a small country's unshakable will to resist,
something may break in the logic of domination of the great
powers; and in this case the small country may force the large one
to retreat, to change its policy.

About a year ago, I happened to ask an important American
official what the United States' interests were in supporting Israel,
and what Israel could do if there were a clash between an American
policy and a vital necessity for Israel. He answered that there were
very few specific interests (which I already knew anyway) and that
it was more a question of general sympathy. Israel was like the
United States in many ways—in its democracy, its pioneering
spirit, and so on. I pointed out to him that in the face of a concrete
policy, diffuse emotions would perhaps not have much weight. He
thought that, even so, the political importance of feelings like these
should not be underestimated. The sympathy aroused by Israel's
fighting for its survival and convincing the American public that
there was a limit to how far one could retreat, was a political factor
in the United States, not so much because of the Jewish vote or the
role of the Jews in American society—which is secondary, in the
end—but because of American public opinion as such. In the long
run, no American government can afford to ignore public opinion.
In this sort of situation, therefore, public opinion is a factor which
must be taken into account.

MAHMOUD HUSSEIN: I am not underestimating in the least the
political importance of so-called emotional factors, or the weight of
public opinion when it is more or less general, because these
elements are now a permanent part of any concrete political
situation. They are evidence of the fact that even when the people
have no power to make decisions, they still have the diffuse,
implicit power to limit, at least in certain ways, the actions of those
who do make the decisions.

In the case of Western public opinion about Israel, we can see
that, more than anything else, it is based on a collective feeling of
guilt about the Jews abandoned by Europe to Hitler during the
Second World War. The pioneering nature of the Zionist *Yishuv*
might also explain the spontaneous affinity that the ordinary

American feels for what he conceives the Israeli to be. But if such considerations exist, if they are part of the political makeup of Western government, they are not, as I see it, determining factors. The American government, for example, generally gives priority to considerations of money, military effectiveness, strategic convenience, rather than sentimental affinities—and public opinion allows it to do this as long as its own interests are not directly hurt by it. To cite only the case of Latin America, it is clear that Americans feel more comfortable with dictatorships than with regimes that are similar to Western democracies.

You spoke of Israel's rejection of the Rogers Plan, which finally led Washington to give it up for a while. But public opinion in America was in no way responsible for the government's changing its mind about this. The change of mind took place because Israel, as we said a moment ago, had a certain leeway for local maneuvering, because of its victory in 1967 and the abrupt weakening of the Arab regimes. This allowed Israel to make the case to Washington that intransigence was more effective than conciliation, that the Arabs would capitulate in the end; and Israel appealed to the Americans' interest in seeing the whole sphere of Soviet influence in the Middle East collapse, which was bound to happen according to this hypothesis.

After 1973 the Rogers Plan came up again, hardly modified; Israel was no longer equal to putting up the same kind of resistance to American demands. Why? Because the balance of forces had been changed—not because the American public had begun to lose interest in Israel. For me there is one event which illustrates the change in the situation quite well. After the cease-fire, as we know, Kissinger asked that the Israelis allow provisions to go through to Egypt's Third Army, which was surrounded on the right bank of the canal. He apparently told Dayan, who was trying to make him change his mind, that if the provisions did not get through, Israel would have to learn to get along by itself. The provisions went through. And to a Knesset which was giving voice to its bitterness, Dayan declared: "I understand what you're saying, but we had no choice." This doesn't mean that we think the United States is tempted, at this point, to impose choices on Israel that would seem suicidal to it. We only want to remark that the Americans are in the process of imposing a form of agreement which corresponds roughly to the arrangements of the Rogers Plan, and which Israel is no longer in a position to reject.

JEAN LACOUTURE: I would like to emphasize that Mahmoud Hussein is referring to a time of war, to a time when arms still counted. In periods like that, the superpowers exert an almost decisive pressure because they control the flow of arms. But when a period of agreements follows the period of arms shipments, the will to independence—as Friedländer described it so well just now—can be expressed far more freely.

MAHMOUD HUSSEIN: There is certainly something special about a period of open hostility. The dependence of the fighters on the source of arms is at its height then. But the cessation of hostilities should not be confused with the cessation of the state of belligerence. The Israelis did not stop arming themselves after October 24th or even stop perfecting their arsenal as fast as they could. They need the United States more and more for credits, military equipment, supplies of all kinds. The difference between today and the month of October 1973 lies in the degree of urgency of this need and not in its essential character. Israel's dependence remains very deep, even after the cease-fire.

But there is something even more serious, I think; it is that the contradictions which have arisen so far between the American line and the Israeli line are going in the wrong direction. America is trying to keep the Arab point of view in mind, while Israel is showing more intransigence. When Friedländer was looking for an example of possible confrontation between the two, what occurred to him was the possibility of contention over Sharm-el-Sheikh, the United States ready to give it back to the Arabs and Israel refusing to do so. There is nothing very encouraging about that. To keep to the example cited, there is not a shadow of a doubt that Sharm-el-Sheikh must be returned to Egypt! So the coming frictions between Washington and Tel Aviv really ought to take another direction.

It is urgent that the Israeli groups who truly want peace begin to conceive of their opposition to American policy in new terms, which would bring it closer to Arab feelings, rather than conceiving of it in terms of an exacerbated nationalism which could alienate them even further from the Arabs while leaving Washington in the permanent role of arbitrator.

SAUL FRIEDLÄNDER: First of all, I don't think the Israelis have any illusions about the decisive power of good will. I simply wanted to emphasize that Israeli policy should not be considered as an obvious extension of American policy, rather that Israel should be seen as a country which is capable of asserting an independent will and one which would use every means at its disposal, particularly obstinate refusal, to oppose the exercise of an American "Diktat," if it ever happened that such a "Diktat" was drawn up, which I obviously hope will not be the case. As for the analysis of the objective differences between American imperialism and the interests of the Israeli people, I am not using the same schemata as you, but this leads me directly to another point of yours.

Yesterday you said that 1973 exposed the real problem at the heart of Arab society and was going to cause profound upheavals. You asked the question: "Won't these upheavals in the Arab countries give rise to similar social upheavals in Israel? Won't there be coinciding upheavals in the two societies?" I think we will be coming back to this at the end of our debate, but I want to say right away that one of the ideas the Israelis have been expressing for a long time—I mean those Israelis who call themselves socialists—is this one: How does it happen that the Arab countries, which have so many domestic problems, attach such importance to Israel? Why don't they concentrate on solving their domestic problems? Israel has never seen itself in the role of a "pawn of imperialism" which would try to interfere with the domestic evolution of the Arab countries—quite the opposite. You might answer me that as long as the problem of Israel was not resolved in one way or another, it wasn't possible to turn to the domestic problems, and this is what you explained to me. In any case, I agree with you that profound tranformations are soon going to take place in your country. Will the same thing happen to us? It is impossible to foretell.

Later on I will try to explain to you how I see the interaction of social forces in Israel. Right now I would like to say this. For you it is possible that from now on social contradictions will take precedence over external problems, or that external problems will be considered in the perspective of the larger domestic problems. For Israel, the domestic problems are real and fundamental, but I don't think I'm wrong in saying that the external problem, or more exactly, the Zionist concept of unity, takes precedence—so far, in any case—over internal dissensions. Whatever the dissensions within Israeli society may be, whatever the social evolution, whatever the opposition to a particular government, whatever the changes of government, and insofar as I know the situation and can analyze it objectively, the maintenance of national unity around the basic idea of a Jewish and Zionist state will still take precedence over any internal problem in the foreseeable future.

I think this is one fundamental difference between the way you see your situation and the way we see ours.

MAHMOUD HUSSEIN: This is exactly what worries us. When you consider Israel's future internal problems, you pose them within the context of permanent national unity. Yet up to the present this unity has been a unity of distrust, of hostility toward the Arabs more than anything else. My hopes for the future depend on being able to break up such forms of unity, to create a gulf between those who want to continue on the trajectory of the past—setting up the Arabs against the Israelis and perpetuating the dependence of both sides on foreign powers—and those who are trying to break this vicious circle. For the moment I am not alluding to the possibility of the de-Zionization of Israel—I'll certainly return to that further on. I would rather talk about a political choice which ought to lead some Israelis to contest your country's present subordination to the United States.

You said—and it was not a slip—that you hoped that no major opposition of interests between Israel and Washington would appear. This is very significant. We hope for this opposition, but opposition in a very particular sense. We hope to see profound antagonisms burst out and turn the people of the region against

Washington's imperialist strategy—antagonisms which for the moment are still far from being entirely evident. We suspect that if the real breath of independence is felt both among the Arabs and among the Israelis, the United States will not like it at all, and we are very eager to trouble the United States in this way. You view the differences between Israel and Washington in a very passive way. Washington is trying to impose something on you that makes you very uneasy. We are accustomed to distrusting Washington, and we see these differences from a much more active, creative point of view.

We hope to overthrow the structures on which America's power and our weakness both rest. This is a goal which, when it is achieved—and unfortunately that won't be in the near future—will represent a major defeat for American imperialism. We don't see how the Israelis can imagine a future similar to ours if they don't hope for this just as much as we do.

SAUL FRIEDLÄNDER: This time, I am speaking for myself and not necessarily as an average Israeli.

There are many Israelis who are farther to the left than I am about domestic questions, and though for them it is conceivable that Israel might detach itself from the American or liberal Western ideological orbit, Israel's Zionist vocation is still essential. I must say that as for me—and I consider myself a liberal and have never considered myself a Marxist in any way—I find nothing distasteful about American society. I can easily see that various aspects of American society must change, but as a type of human society I find it acceptable. It is a kind of society which I would be willing to see develop in Israel, because it is a liberal society, with all the positive qualities that that implies. I also know the negative aspects of it, but I prefer it to a so-called egalitarian society. These are my political options, but in Israel there are socialists who would, I think, like to see a movement grow up that would take an almost revolutionary direction, while remaining at the same time dedicated to the Zionist ideal.

MAHMOUD HUSSEIN: Your attitude is shared by many Arabs, who would like to bring about a society based on the American model.

Except that it would actually be impossible to build an American society in an Arab world. Because, first of all, to us American society does not represent a model of liberalism and tolerance but an oppressive force intent on plundering our wealth and relying on the consolidation of conservative forces in the Arab world to help in this intention; but also because Arab societies are very inegalitarian, and because the class forces which have been influenced by the Western life style and who hope to see it achieved in the Arab world constitute a series of privileged minorities.

The overwhelming majority of the Arab population—which contains the forces of profound, structural change for society—is attached to a system of values, to ways of thinking, working, organizing, which certainly have to be revolutionized in order to allow the people to master the problems of present-day society, but which cannot be revolutionized on an imported model—whether American or Soviet—but only from within, spurred on by the creative impulse of the Arab people themselves, by methods which will have to be both authentic and innovative and which actually still remain to be discovered. At this level there is certainly an important difference between the Arab societies and Israeli society—Israeli society can aspire to follow the American model, but by so doing it will accentuate its strangeness, its externality to the Arab world.

It should be said in passing that the American model we are talking about does not have much to do with the pioneer society of the seventeenth century. Ask the American blacks what they think about this. You cannot ignore all the inequalities that are taken for granted within the meshes of liberalism, including racism.

One last word. You say that the Israelis are wondering how it happens that the Arab people, who have so many domestic problems to solve, are so preoccupied by the confrontation with Israel. But Israel *is* a domestic problem for the Arabs! Its armies are actually inside vast Arab territories, and until October 1973 Israel made us very aware of how much influence it had on the course of our political life.

In Jordan, for example, several times during 1969 and 1970, you declared that you would not allow King Hussein to be overthrown, and that if he was, you would occupy the East Bank of the River Jordan. Your interventions in Lebanon can't be kept track of any longer; and Sharon boasted that he could intervene in Baghdad or Tripoli whenever he wanted to. This being the case, how can you expect that the confrontation with you will not take precedence over all other considerations?

It is true that things today are not exactly the same. The Egyptians and the Syrians have reason to think that they will regain their territories. But that is not enough. There is the question of recognizing the Palestinians. It seems that many Israelis are still blinding themselves to this issue and hoping that by some sort of miracle it will vanish into thin air. This is a dangerous illusion, because from now on this issue will be one of the preoccupations of the Arab people. Both Egyptians and Syrians certainly want to see the conflict end, but the conflict will not be over until the Palestinians are no longer exiles. That is why it is necessary to emphasize the fact—if it has not emerged sufficiently from everything that has gone before—that all the prospects for the future envisioned so far must remain suspended for the time being, and that we find ourselves in a transitional period which will not end until the territories occupied in 1967 are restored and Palestinian sovereignty is recognized. Without this, everything gained in October 1973 may still be thwarted, if not actually challenged again.

The Range of Arab Diversity

JEAN LACOUTURE: Before coming to the question of Palestine, which is an important element in the Arab-Israeli situation, it would be good if Mahmoud Hussein described the range of Arab diversity for us, and told us how the war of 1973 either increased the number of different movements and attitudes within the Arab world, or unified them.

MAHMOUD HUSSEIN: It is true that I have tended to make the different attitudes seem the same in this dialogue in order to simplify my account. Yet there are almost as many official positions on the Israeli question as there are Arab governments, not to mention the various positions taken by particular political movements or social classes that are not represented in the governments.

However, we should try to isolate the dominant lines of power, the principal tendencies, so that we can orient ourselves in the midst of this diversity of attitudes. Very briefly, let us say that from 1967 to 1973 the two principal movements that had divided the Arab world until then slowly approached one another. One centered around Nasser and was nationalist, "progressive," favored state ownership, and was attempting to free the region from foreign supervision by playing one superpower against the other. The other movement was pro-capitalist and pro-West, and its main advocate was Saudi Arabia's King Faisal, who was hoping for close alliance with the United States.

The 1967 defeat induced these two movements, in spite of their strong mutual distrust, to coordinate their policies little by little in the face of Israel's challenge, though it must be said that this coordination did not become really effective until after Nasser's death, with the clearly liberal and pro-American leaning of Egyptian policy under Sadat. Syria under Assad joined these two, not without certain reservations at first, and from then on they sought more and more actively to establish an Arab-Israeli dialogue based on regaining American friendship and allowing Soviet influence to become weaker.

Opposed to this movement were the so-called diehards, who rejected even the idea of a dialogue with Israel. But among them we must distinguish two tendencies: one that was nationalist and somewhat chauvinistic, represented by the Libyan and Iraqi leaders, whose policy was an extension of the traditional view of the problem, which we decribed yesterday; and a second movement, or rather bundle of movements—radical or revolutionary—made up of young people from all the Arab countries, mostly students.

One last word about the special position of Algeria. Boumédienne kept up his contacts with all the movements I have mentioned, and also with all the countries who were at odds with one another—the United States and France, the USSR and China, Libya and Cuba, and so forth. This put him in an excellent position at the moment when the conflict broke out, though his role was not crucial.

October 1973 changed the relations among the different movements. The ones in favor of making peace, who up to that point had been on the defensive and had felt more and more threatened, regained some degree of initiative; the chauvinistic "diehards," who had been speaking up very loudly until the month of October, were obliged to lower their voices. They are relatively out of phase now, and have no real alternative to propose.

As for the radical and revolutionary movements, though the war took them somewhat by surprise, it also led them to draw certain important conclusions. Their attitudes are not at all unified—there is no single Arab people's organization—but they essentially agree about the need to become more and more concerned with the political and economic conditions of the working classes, in order to regain our fundamental national rights. They are pretty much convinced that as a result of this approach, the revolutionary forces of the future will not be formed in the course of a popular war against Israel, as a number of us thought before 1973, but rather in the course of internal struggles for basic democracy and new social relations. Once again, and I hope for the last time, I am leaving the Palestinians aside.

To finish up, I want to mention a political attitude that may grow stronger among the Arab bourgeoisie in the future—it is Boumédienne's attitude and it has a good deal in common with arguments advanced by the Egyptian journalist Hassanein Heikal just after the war. It is a harder position than those of Faisal, Sadat and Assad, while at the same time remaining "realistic." Its premise is the need for a unified Arab policy at the diplomatic and military levels and especially at the economic level—a policy which would allow the Arab world as a whole to play a new role in the world, a role that would be more autonomous and more effective, and that would above all enable it to resist American pressure while dealing not only with Russians but also as much as possible with the Common Market countries and Japan.

JEAN LACOUTURE: What is surprising, Mahmoud Hussein, is that in the end, the contradictions which put you in opposition to the present Arab leaders, whom you qualify as bourgeois, seem rather few from the description you have given us of the situation.

Probably with good reason, you describe the initiative taken on 6 October 1973 by these leaders, Sadat and Assad, as an attempt to keep control over the popular forces and remain in a powerful position, and also attract the great powers, particularly the Americans. An objective that is therefore more conservative than revolutionary. But what follows in your account no longer places you in "antagonistic" contradiction, in a class struggle with the present Arab powers. This is a little baffling to me, and perhaps to Friedländer too...

MAHMOUD HUSSEIN: That's quite right. The increase in socially conservative tendencies, which characterized the period following October 1973, contains the seeds of a class struggle which will no doubt go further than it has up to now—as anti-Israel preoccupations weigh less and less heavily on the expression of domestic needs. But this burden will have to be lifted—otherwise the possibilities for a fight for radical transformations will remain nothing more than possibilities, dreams, aspirations, almost completely stifled by Israel's persistent challenge.

This is what leads me to characterize the present period as a period of transition, whose prospects are still contradictory and uncertain. Until Israel answers the two demands—to withdraw from the occupied territories and recognize Palestinian sovereignty—in a decisive way, the united anti-Israel front will remain, the regimes which started the October war will continue to exercise the popular authority they have acquired, and the masses will continue to be thwarted in their struggle against the conservative Arab interests. The Arabs have no choice but to stay together on the same side of the barricades until this period of transition is over.

SAUL FRIEDLÄNDER: Your analysis raises still one more question.

When you mentioned the few "diehards" in Arab society, you seemed to be implying that they did not represent anything very important. Leaving aside the groups that draw their inspiration from revolutionary slogans or from an essentially pro-Palestine point of view, don't you think extremist tendencies like Qaddafi's have strong reverberations in Egypt? And couldn't one say that there is a militant sector in Egypt (which doesn't necessarily use the issue of Palestine as a rallying cry) that is actually larger than you seem to be saying it is?

MAHMOUD HUSSEIN: Qaddafi is a special case. His speeches can only be understood if they are put back into their original context, the strictly orthodox Islam in which spiritual matters are still fundamental, in which Islam is synonymous with a certain concept of social justice which aims to be rigorous but is sometimes despotic. This produces a strange mixture of elements that is rather out of place amid the class realities and the requirements of modern international diplomacy, and that is really why Qaddafi appears as an eccentric who disturbs many people and may inspire some people, but who is still a special case.

Before 1973, there was response to his message everywhere, including certain popular Moslem sectors of Egypt. In a language which the people understood, he touched responsive chords; he denounced Sadat's hesitation about Israel, the weight of bureaucracy, and the ostentatious increase in wealth of the bourgeoisie while the masses were making heavy material sacrifices for the sake of a war of liberation which was still only a mirage. The Libyan statements were magnificently incoherent. Sometimes they pictured the Jews as brothers, "men of the Book," and sometimes as the enemies of Islam; sometimes they represented the United States as the cruelest kind of imperialist and sometimes as a rampart of religion against Soviet atheism—and so forth. But that did not matter very much. Compared to the immobility and lack of imagination of the other Arab politicians, Qaddafi's fieriness was effective, and all the more effective since he was far from the battlefield and no one could call him to account or find out how much his speeches were actually worth.

After 1973 his influence declined sharply. Not only had he lost the political initiative, but at the very moment his rivals were wresting it from him on the battlefield, he committed an unpardonable tactical error: he criticized them publicly, casting doubt on the war, on its objectives, on the way it had been started. This was perhaps due to the fact that he had not been consulted about it, but the consequences were disastrous for him. Today no movement in Egypt feels it has anything in common with him—perhaps some miniscule and marginal groups, but no important ones.

So that when you ask me if the "diehards" did not have deep roots in Egypt, the facts themselves are sufficient answer. The left wing students who constituted the main opposition to the regime before 1973, and who go furthest in their radical attitude toward the war against Israel, are anti-Qaddafi, even the religious ones—for there does exist a Left which is neither atheist nor Marxist. In any case they are unanimous in believing that the principal outside enemy is American imperialism and that even though Israel is closely tied to it, it could still gain admission to the Middle East if it changed its orientation and recognized the Arabs' national rights.

JEAN LACOUTURE: Let us try to be more precise, more specific about Egypt to begin with. One organization has always been notorious for its fundamental antagonism towards Israel—the Moslem Brotherhood. Nasser certainly broke up its power, but the movement is still alive. A resurgence of the Islamic feeling has been taking place around Sadat and Hatem, who themselves have been sympathizers with the Moslem Brotherhood for a long time, and this feeling played quite an active role in favor of expulsion of the Russians. The Brotherhood is made up of the leading citizens of provincial society, who twine beads around their fingers and build mosques and banks at the same time, and are much closer to the center of power than they were in Nasser's time. Couldn't we find camouflaged among them the same "diehard" tendencies?

And we should not forget Mohammed Hassanein Heikal, Nasser's "alter ego," whom Sadat did not want to associate with. Naturally I don't consider him an extremist, a warmonger against Israel; but it is conceivable that he poses a problem, if only because of his ties with Qaddafi.

There remains the army. General Shazli, the "war hero" of October, has become a national figure. Isn't it true that his dismissal increased his prestige? Couldn't he be seen as a sort of Egyptian Dayan who might one day ally himself with the forces of the extreme right and become an alternative to Sadat?

MAHMOUD HUSSEIN: We should agree on the meaning of the term "diehard." If it is taken to mean the wish to destroy Israel, we don't think there is any diehard movement in Egypt today. In the hearts of some people there may be a wound which is not healing and which could be opened again by one of the national chauvinist groups—what is left of the Moslem Brotherhood, for example. As far as I know there isn't much left of it.

Naturally, these movements may grow stronger, gain a wider audience, if the Israeli leaders prevent a solution that the Arabs would find honorable, but let me repeat that I do not see any truly representative movement in the Egyptian political spectrum that demands the destruction of Israel.

Then what is this provincial and traditional bourgeoisie, who are these lovers of beads and banks that are surrounding Sadat? They are as liberal in their views on the economy as they are conservative politically. More than anything else they want to reactivate the private sector, reopen the country to the Western market. They know that at this point what the Egyptian banks need above all is a long period of calm at the borders, and they hope to establish the prosperity of their businesses on this. In any case, there won't be any Arab or American investors until they feel reassured on this subject. Moreover, this was one of the important reasons for Sadat's making conciliatory proposals to Israel before October 1973. In the present context, the traditionalism of this part of the bourgeoisie is just the opposite of the diehard tendency.

As for Heikal, he is a good spokesman for the other part of the Egyptian bourgeoisie, which is in competition with the first—the new state bourgeoisie; it is composed mainly of technocrats, the natural sons of Nasserism who would like to preserve at least a part of the heritage—which is to say, they would like to modernize the national economy and make it more flexible without questioning the priority of the public sector. They are in favor of rapprochement with the United States but would like it to be more cautious, to counterbalance the dialogue with the USSR rather than cut if off. What they hope for most of all, now, is an Arab economic power that would deal with Western Europe in particular, offering choice assets: oil, dollars, and a great hunger for modernization. They are secretly thinking of what Heikal wrote before he was kicked out: Sadat was too quick to trust the Americans and he broke up the movement of Arab solidarity that had formed in October.

But it is still only a matter of nuances between Heikal and Sadat; there is certainly a significant difference between their points of view, but they both agree on a solution to the Arab-Israeli conflict that would grant a place to Israel if it was no longer a threat.

I can't say anything precise about the case of General Shazli. I think he is still popular in Egypt and that he may still have a part to play. Everyone knows that in October he wanted the Egyptian army to continue to advance after the Bar-Lev line was taken. But as far as I know, he never thought of penetrating into the Negev, not even at some time in the future.

> JEAN LACOUTURE: Let's go on to talk about Syria. Don't you think that in Damascus the debate is still open and that the unyielding Ba'ath movement headed first by Salah Jadid and then by General Assad, who is more moderate, is a permanent, highly motivated, and powerful opponent of negotiations and lasting settlement with Israel?

MAHMOUD HUSSEIN: Of course, as we pass from Egypt to Syria the resistance to a change of strategic perspective is much stronger; there are many more tensions and the pitch of feeling is much higher.

It is said that the intention of Assad and of the majority in the leadership of the Syrian Ba'ath is to join Sadat and Faisal in seeking some kind of peaceful solution. The war of October, followed by the war of attrition on the Golan Heights, gave Assad the national prestige he needed in order to make the sudden change in policy that was condemned by his opponents as a betrayal. But what he is trying to do is much more difficult here than it would be in Egypt, because the feelings of frustration about Israel are deeper and more intense here. If the Israeli leaders continue to be intransigent for much longer on the question of withdrawal from the part of the Golan Heights that is still occupied or on the question of Palestinian national rights, his position will unquestionably be threatened.

In the course he has chosen to take he has, at the moment, the support of the United States and the USSR, and the very considerable help of Egypt and Saudi Arabia; within Syria he can count on the support of the petit bourgeois, who are hoping for an improvement in their position, and probably also a section of the proletariat, who want to win the rights which were withheld for too long because of the sacrifices demanded by the preparations for war.

It should also be pointed out that Syria's society is more heterogeneous than Egypt's, and less unified ideologically. There are cities that are still very traditionalist, not to mention parts of the countryside; there are also the historic animosities between the Sunnis and the Shiahs, and all this can be turned to account by the enemies of President Assad. Yet it does not seem to us that in the present situation they have any coherent alternative to offer or that they represent an immediate danger to him.

SAUL FRIEDLÄNDER: Your analysis implies that there may be sudden changes in Syria because of its unstable situation and because of the relative strength of the groups opposed to a settlement with Israel. What do you think will happen if there are upheavals in Syria which lead to its withdrawal from negotiations, whether because of internal problems or because of the pressure from the Soviet Union? Do you think the movement in Egypt which favors negotiation is powerful enough for Egypt to continue to negotiate alone?

MAHMOUD HUSSEIN: The problem cannot be posed that way. We have remarked that there were large differences among the situations of the Arab ruling forces involved in the conflict. But we have also remarked that there existed a larger movement that transcended these differences and carried all the ruling forces toward negotiation. If the situation in Syria changed abruptly, it would probably mean that relations between the Arabs and the Israelis had degenerated to such an extent that the balance on which this policy depended would be upset, not only in Syria but in all the countries concerned. The supporters of negotiation in Egypt would certainly be in very poor position then. It would be more than an isolated incident; it would be the beginning of a chain reaction brought on by the degeneration of the climate in general.

SAUL FRIEDLÄNDER: This is obviously a problem that worries the Israelis. That is why many people are saying: "After all, concessions are dangerous because some day the extremists will take power again in one of the neighboring countries and will block off all the others. No matter what you do, there is always one weak link in the chain and the whole process of negotiation will suffer from it." Others answer: "No, Egypt is not necessarily turned only toward the Arab world. Egypt is a special case." This attitude is reflected in the idea that comes up often these days—to negotiate with Egypt first. The Syrians might change their minds. We must therefore come to an agreement with the Egyptians, even at the risk of remaining in conflict with the others. We are leaving the Palestinian problem aside for the moment, and referring only to states. Does separate negotiation with Egypt seem possible to you? Does it seem conceivable to you that Egypt might go its own way for its own reasons, saying to itself that after all if the Syrian "diehards" have forced Assad out of the negotiations, that is the Syrians' business, but Egypt, for domestic reasons, will go its own way?

MAHMOUD HUSSEIN: I don't believe that Egypt can go its own way and I am truly astonished that any one in Israel can have any illusions about this. Look at what happened during the war of attrition on the Golan Heights. A growing uneasiness appeared in Egypt, in the army just as much as in the rest of the country, and this uneasiness could be summed up in one question: "Is Sadat going to let Syria fall? We entered the war together. We must come out of it together..." This emphasized the attitude which Heikal defended within the Egyptian bourgeoisie—he felt that we had to continue to pose the Arab-Israeli problem in a total way and refuse to break it up state by state.

SAUL FRIEDLÄNDER: But then, in your opinion, in the opinion of the Arabs, how total is total? If you say it includes only the countries at war, I can understand; that would involve only the countries that border on Israel. But if you say it includes the whole of the Arab world, then, in the end, everything would hinge on the intransigence of Faisal or Qaddafi, or on the Iraqis.

MAHMOUD HUSSEIN: No, it includes essentially Egypt, Syria, and Palestine. Officially, of course, it also includes Jordan and Lebanon. But let me tell you that the fear inspired in you by our "diehards" provokes me to ask you a similar question: "What about the Likud? The Zionist 'diehards' who absolutely refuse to abandon the West Bank? What will we do if they end up seizing power from the present anomalous coalition?''

Clearly, the position of the Syrian "diehards" is strengthened by the existence of the Israeli "diehards" and vice versa, but the Israeli diehards are far more threatening to the peace. Why? Because their spokesmen are not marginal figures like Salah Jadid or leaders who are outside the area of direct confrontation, like Qaddafi. Their spokesmen constitute a group of powerful parties that command a large minority of the Israeli electorate, and who have friends as powerful as Dayan in the very heart of the ruling coalition. The Israeli diehards are two steps away from power. That is not the case with us.

The Question of Borders

JEAN LACOUTURE: It would seem that now is a good time to pass on to the facts of the Arab-Israeli situation itself—its main features, its basic structure, and the prospects for solution, particularly in regard to the question of borders. Friedländer has the floor.

SAUL FRIEDLÄNDER: I will try to sum up briefly the elements of the official Israeli position, and then will give some personal ideas which are not entirely opposed to the official position (if they were, my purely subjective remarks would have little interest). It does not seem out of the question to me that sooner or later these kinds of ideas will be accepted, at least in part. They are in the air and would allow us to resolve certain dilemmas.

The official position, for the time being, is as follows (we are dealing here with the question of the borders between Israel and the Arab states, and I am intentionally putting aside the Palestinian problem, which will be an entire subject in itself): No major withdrawal until negotiations for a definitive settlement have begun—after the cease-fire there were some withdrawals, but as you have pointed out, they were not very extensive. We are now coming to the decisive stage of negotiations for a final settlement, in other words to the problem of permanent borders. Israel has always officially declared itself ready to give back a substantial part of the occupied territories, more or less in the following manner—although there could be variations as a result of diplomatic talks: Israel would return the major portion of the Sinai Peninsula, with the exception of a small coastal strip which would link the Mediterranean coast with Sharm-el-Sheikh, since this is an important strategic point. Territorial continuity between Israel and Sharm-el-Sheikh would have to be assured by a coastal strip along the Red Sea. For the time being, Israel does not want to withdraw from the Golan Heights (although a few small exceptions to this have been made—Kuneitra, for example, has been abandoned, and this might be followed by some other minor withdrawals). But, the heights are very narrow, and as you know, they overlook a densely populated valley, with kibbutzim established almost at the very edge. To withdraw would mean exposing ouselves once again to danger of Syrian shellings if things ever took a turn for the worse.

Concerning the West Bank, the idea accepted by most members of the government and by the majority of the people is that Israel will return about three-quarters of it, keeping a neck of land that will descend the length of the Jordan Valley, thus giving the Jordanians—or the Palestinians—the free use of a passage to the Jericho area, and that way guaranteeing territorial continuity between Jordan and the parts of the West Bank that would be given back, but at the same time allowing Israel to close off this passage if hostilities ever began again. Israel would keep the city of Jerusalem and its surroundings, possibly extended to Hebron by a strip of territory.

All the territories given back would be demilitarized, which means that no Egyptian troops would be stationed in the Sinai and no Jordanian or Palestinian troops would be allowed on the West Bank with heavy weapons. Any infraction of this demilitarization would unquestionably be a *casus belli* for Israel.

We can summarize this plan by saying that the major concern is for long-term security, based on a few limited annexations of territory, which would be carried out in such a way as to ensure a minimal annexation of populations.

Israel has been mentioning this plan since 1968. If a conference of Arab heads of state announced tomorrow that this plan was acceptable, one could say, without great risk, that the very same evening Israel would sign a peace treaty. But we have not reached that point, and this plan is really no more than a basis for discussion, since, officially, the Israelis are going to the negotiating table without any preestablished plan at all. Officially, there are no preconditions, everything is open to discussion. As someone said, even Tel Aviv can be discussed. Obviously, Tel Aviv is not going to be given up, but everything is subject to negotiation; there is not one detail that cannot be called into question during the negotiations. That is the official position insofar as we can know it.

JEAN LACOUTURE: You spoke of Tel Aviv, which hardly concerns us here, but not of Jerusalem, which is much more pertinent. . .

SAUL FRIEDLÄNDER: I mentioned it, but would like to go into greater detail. In this official plan, a *sine qua non* for the moment is Israeli sovereignty over Jerusalem. In the eyes of the Israeli government, the question of Jerusalem cannot be opened, since Jerusalem was officially annexed a few days after the Six Day War. Obviously, all sorts of questions can be raised. What about the Arab part of Jerusalem? What about the holy places? One could consider giving extraterritorial status to rather large areas, including the holy places and the Arab sections of the city, over which Israel would have no legal claim to sovereignty, and which would thus be placed under Jordanian control. Officially, however, Jerusalem is not negotiable.

MAHMOUD HUSSEIN: Don't you think there is a contradiction between saying that the Israeli government is ready to discuss everything, even Tel Aviv, and the plan that you have just presented to us, which excludes so many things from discussion?

SAUL FRIEDLÄNDER: When we say that "we are ready to discuss everything," we are stating a general formula, which no one really believes in. But obviously the Arabs can take the Israeli government at its word, come to Geneva, and discuss Jerusalem. . . There is no doubt about that. Theoretically, nothing prevents them from asking again: "What about Galilee?" "What about the 1947 borders?'' Israel would answer. Theoretically, Israel's idea is let's negotiate.

JEAN LACOUTURE: Allow me to look back for a moment and add a slight but interesting detail to the record. During a long conversation with General Dayan in Tel Aviv about four years ago, I heard him say: ''We would like to have settlements of people on the West Bank, but we can also very easily envisage Jordanian settlements on what is now Israeli territory. It is possible, then, that an Arab flag could fly over certain parts of Israel...'' This is hardly feasible, but it proves that all sorts of ideas are possible...

SAUL FRIEDLÄNDER: I would like to pick up on what Jean Lacouture has just said, since in today's issue of *Le Monde*, 26 July 1974, I saw a declaration by General Dayan in favor of the initiative of the one hundred and fifty people who have just tried to establish a new settlement near Nablus. According to him, these settlements of people must be encouraged, no matter what the ultimate political solution or political destiny of the region. His idea is the following: Whatever the final border might be, there is no reason why Jews should not live on the other side, under the Jordanian government or possibly the Palestinian government, and the same for Arabs in Israel. At first glance this idea might seem a bit curious, but after a moment of reflection, it seems fundamentally right. It implies that the region from now on should be an integrated whole.

MAHMOUD HUSSEIN: But you just said that the plan in question is an attempt to keep the annexation of populations to a minimum.

SAUL FRIEDLÄNDER: Yes, but not everything is logical in this business and everyone has his own ideas. Each Israeli has at least four political solutions to offer. And yet, why are there propositions of this kind? Because of the holy places. There is a Jewish holy place at Hebron; the city of Jericho is of great Biblical importance; and if people want to live near Hebron or Jericho, this should be taken into account—it would only be a question of a few dozen or a few hundred people living there under Jordanian sovereignty, for example. And if a group of Arabs really wanted to settle near Haifa, they should be allowed to do so. In each case, if it were a question of massive migrations, the idea would be in contradiction to the refusal to annex large populations.

MAHMOUD HUSSEIN: This is not a minor point. We have nothing against the principle of Jews living among the Arabs, but coming from Dayan such a proposal raises legitimate suspicions. We have only to think about the manner in which the Zionist *Yishuv* developed—little bits of territory embedded in the Arab world that gradually expanded until all of Palestine was taken over. This reminds us of the popular story of Goha's nail. Goha has just sold his house and asks the buyers not to pull out a certain nail that he is very fond of. They leave the nail in place, and Goha keeps coming back, usually at meal times, to come in and have a look at his nail. After a little while he's living in his house again, and he has all the profits from the transaction in his pocket as well.

SAUL FRIEDLÄNDER: But if this were what he had in mind, Dayan would not say: "No matter what the political future of these regions might be." He understands very well that the Jews living under a Jordanian regime, or possibly a Palestinian regime, would not have complete freedom over their actions and movements.

MAHMOUD HUSSEIN: But what if there were disagreements over the status of the Jews in the areas in question? You have just said that these areas, in the eyes of the Israeli government, must be demilitarized. If there were a dispute, wouldn't the Israeli army be in a good position to intervene in a way that would always be favorable to the Jewish population?

SAUL FRIEDLÄNDER: I don't think it's worth our while to spend time discussing other people's opinions, especially General Dayan's. In any case, he is not a member of the present government, and his position today is at the extreme end of the official position. We began speaking about his opinions in an indirect way; they are not all necessarily logical. His basic idea is that in this part of the region—especially the territory that represents ancient Palestine—

an economic, political and even human coexistence should be established among the various groups and states. These are propositions that should not be rejected *a priori*, because, paradoxically, they link up with the idea of the Palestinians' "Democratic State," only in a completely different form. I'm joking when I say this, but not completely. In both cases the notion emerges of *coexistence at the heart of a wider space*. Dayan obviously doesn't support the idea of the Palestinian democratic state; he expresses the notion of coexistence in another manner. But the basic notion that we can see in both approaches, no matter how contrary they may be, is that there is no longer any place for absolute barriers between Israelis and Arabs in this part of the Middle East.

MAHMOUD HUSSEIN: The principle of fundamental solutions, of new formulas concerning these questions, is wholly admirable. The problem is Dayan's proposition in terms of the present situation.

SAUL FRIEDLÄNDER: If you will allow me to, I would like to sketch my own ideas about these matters. They are completely personal, but they are somehow in the air, and it is for this reason that I bring them up now.

We must begin with the following principles: Israel has a right to guarantees of security, and a right to feel that once a settlement has been concluded conditions will be such that they will not arouse fears of aggression again. Israel has a right to a settlement that assures peace in security.

On the other hand, I well understand, as do many others, that there will be no settlement if we try to occupy Arab territories beyond the 1967 borders which would be significant either in terms of their extent or their historical importance.

Finally, and this is the third element of the problem, we are faced with a conflict that has very deep roots. The mistrust and hostility will not disappear in a day.

The signing of a first agreement will not resolve everything; brotherhood will not suddenly be established in the Middle East. We therefore have a long-term problem of gradual changes in attitudes, and this is not unrelated to the problem of security.

Now, then, can we imagine a settlement that would solve all

these various difficulties? We can conceive of the following plan. *In principle* Israel does not annex any Arab territories beyond the 1967 borders—we will return to the question of Jerusalem later, which is a problem *sui generis*—but the settlement itself must be carried out over a certain length of time. It is by gradually withdrawing from the occupied territories that relations between the two parties will be gradually normalized. There is a phrase in English that expresses this quite well: "A piece of peace for a piece of territory."

To make things more concrete, let us take the case of Egypt. First Israel would formally agree to withdraw from the whole of the Sinai, according to the settlement process I'm going to describe and on the condition, of course, that this process unfolds as predicted. The declaration would be followed by the actual withdrawal from a large part of the Sinai—for example, as far as the al-Arish/Sharm-el-Sheikh line. In turn, Egypt would make a declaration of non-belligerence toward Israel and would guarantee the free passage of Israeli ships through the Suez Canal.

Next, a sort of cooperative surveillance of the evacuated area, using troops from both sides, would be established. Third, Egypt would take another step toward reconciliation by opening its borders to tourists and allowing certain exchanges, and at that moment Israel would make another withdrawal, keeping only Sharm-el-Sheikh. Finally, Egypt would declare itself to be at peace with Israel and would agree—why not?—to exchange commercial or diplomatic missions. Israel would then withdraw from the rest of the Sinai.

A process of this type can be speeded up or slowed down according to the circumstances, but in any case, it is a question of the gradual normalization of relations, in which the time factor plays an important role. In my mind, it could not be accomplished in a few months, but would take several years.

It is clear, moreover, that as relations begin to normalize, the problem of security will become less and less obsessive. The two phenomena are linked in the same way that the parts of a slide rule are contained within one another and move only in relation to one another. I will add another element that seems very important to me. Parallel to all of this, it is necessary to establish more and more cooperative enterprises. There must be more than just the usual activities, such as the exchange of goods and the opening of borders to travelers; there should be enterprises that are sufficiently large and complex to bring together the advanced technologies of both countries in joint efforts that would be pursued in such a way as to make it difficult to move backward and bring about a new conflict.

You remember Johnston's plan, which was based on the short-lived and rather limited idea that Syria, Lebanon, Jordan, and Israel could share the waters of the Jordan and its tributaries. In itself this was a good idea, but it wasn't ambitious enough. Along these lines we can think of much greater possibilities, particularly ones in which nuclear technology is involved.

To sum up, I would say: In principle, no annexation, but a gradual movement toward total nonannexation coordinated with a gradual détente between the Arabs and Israel.

The time factor is equally decisive under these conditions, considering the deep roots of the conflict. For the tensions to ease up, time is needed. Time is the central and fundamental element of this whole idea. Only time will allow for the total withdrawal demanded by the Arabs since 1967 and for an adequate and increasing security for Israel within the 1967 borders. It doesn't matter whether it takes two years, five years, or ten years.

JEAN LACOUTURE: If I understand you correctly, you feel that the process you have just described for Egypt and the Sinai could also be applied to the West Bank and the Golan Heights?

SAUL FRIEDLÄNDER: Yes, that's right.

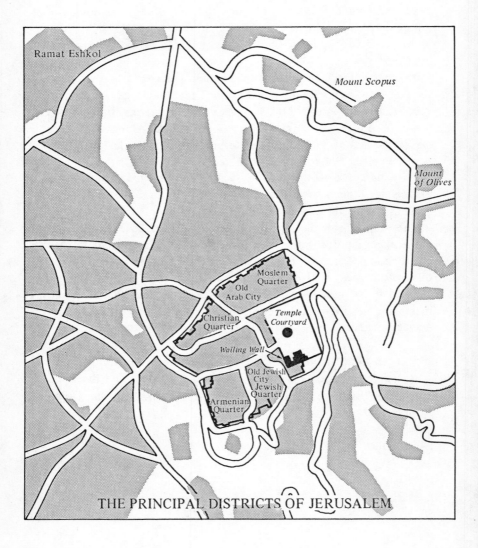

Ramat Eshkol

Mount Scopus

Mount
of Olives

Moslem
Quarter

Old
Arab City

Christian
Quarter

Temple
Courtyard

Wailing Wall

Old Jewish
City
Jewish
Quarter

Armenian
Quarter

THE PRINCIPAL DISTRICTS OF JERUSALEM

Jerusalem

JEAN LACOUTURE: Without interrupting the flow of the discussion, do you think you could say something about Jerusalem?

SAUL FRIEDLÄNDER: This is the most difficult problem of all.

I remember a conversation I had in 1968 with a very intelligent man who was highly informed about Israel's relations with its neighbors—Jacob Herzog, director general of the prime minister's office, who has since died. He feared at that time, he told me, that even if we managed to solve all our problems with the Arabs, Jerusalem, the city of peace, would be the stumbling block in this process to achieve peace. Why? Because all the problems that I have just described have logical solutions, and in the end do not involve deep emotions, at least on the part of the Israelis. The Sinai is a matter of security, of strategy, the Golan Heights as well— there is no one in Israel who feels deep emotional or religious ties with it; the West Bank represents a more complicated problem, but the majority of the population is prepared for an almost complete withdrawal in the long run. Again, it is simply a problem of security.

With Jerusalem, on the other hand, the question is not one of strategy or politics. The whole weight of religious feeling, of aspirations that are thousands of years old, must be taken into consideration: "If I forget thee, O Jerusalem, let my right hand

forget her cunning." It is not "next year in Eretz Yisrael" that the
Jews have said over the centuries, but "next year in Jerusalem."

Now, for the Arabs the situation is the same. It is not just any
city, but the third holy city, a city of considerable emotional
importance. For King Faisal, for example, Jerusalem is the most
important question of all. It is more significant than all the other
occupied territories.

Now, I don't think I'm wrong in saying that for the majority of
Israelis, to give back even a part of Jerusalem is inconceivable.
Resistance of this sort—no matter how irrational it might appear to
be on the surface—becomes a political act in itself. So we should
not deceive ourselves about the enormity of the problem, and yet,
the solution does not seem out of reach. Before anything else, I
think, the following point must be agreed on. The city can no
longer be cut in two; it is an organic, living whole. I don't think
that anyone would object to this idea. The problem is to know
where the sovereignty of each group ends. What I am about to say
may not be obvious, nor even acceptable to the majority of Israelis,
but it seems to me to be a reasonable approach. Jerusalem is
divided into several parts: The new Jewish part, which was an
Israeli city before the 1967 war—there is no problem here, it is
Israel, the capital of Israel. Then you have the Jewish section of the
Old City, which extends to the Wailing Wall—it was a Jewish
quarter for centuries, and remained so until the Jordanians took
control of it during the 1948 war. It is clear—and there is not the
slightest doubt about this for anyone—that Israel will keep this
sector. So we have the new city which makes up the capital and the
Jewish Old City which, from a religious point of view, is something essentially Jewish and sacred to anyone with religious or even
purely emotional ties to the place. Then come the other specifically
Jewish quarters—Ramat Eshkol, Mount Scopus, of course, which
has always been under Israeli control, an enclave in Jordanian
territory (trucks brought supplies to it once a week), and the Mount
of Olives. There exist, then, sectors that are clearly Jewish and
clearly tied to the Jewish historical and religious past. I don't think
that there can be much discussion over Israel's right to maintain
sovereignty over these sectors.

But what about the part that is essentially Arab, the Arab Old

City? I think that this area of Jerusalem should be tied to the Arab part of Palestine, whether it is a Jordanian or Palestinian state. It should be under Arab control, because after all, emotionally and historically, it is part of the Arab world. I don't see why we should insist on maintaining sovereignty over these quarters.

Curiously, the insoluble problem is limited to an area of a few hundred square yards. It is the esplanade where the two great mosques, al-Aqsa and Omar, are located—but it is also the esplanade of the Temple for the Jews, and it is bounded by the Wailing Wall. It is the holy of holies for the Moslem religion. It is the center of all emotions for both groups. It is clear that each of the two groups would like to control this esplanade and thus preserve its religious and historic patrimony.

I must confess that I am hard put to think of a solution to this problem, and I feel that everyone involved must make an enormous effort of imagination. The only reasonable answer, in my opinion, *is that this esplanade be placed under the sovereign control of both groups*, that some kind of joint religious committee, composed of religious leaders from both groups, take on the responsibility of the area.

We are, of course, in the realm of the irrational, but when people kill or are prepared to be killed, it is usually for the sake of an irrational idea. All people, wherever they may be.

JEAN LACOUTURE: For the sake of the discussion, I will try to sum up briefly what I would call the "Friedländer plan" for Jerusalem—which, to someone in a neutral position, as I am, seems fair and reasonable.

On the one hand, keep the old Jewish city of Jerusalem in the State of Israel; on the other hand, take down the sort of Berlin Wall that the Jordanian state created, and transform Jerusalem into an open city, with Israeli sovereignty over the new city and the Jewish Old City. Arab sovereignty (which needs to be elaborated) would be exercised over the part of old Jerusalem with Arab-Moslem traditions. Finally, for the several hundred square yards that constitute the "holy places" for the three great monotheistic religions, a joint religious administration.

Is this coexistence of sovereignties impossible? After all, Berlin lived for many years in this way (1945–1961), even when the hostility between the two Germanies was very active. Two peoples with old resentments can coexist in a single city. You can't say that things ended very well in Berlin, but there is no historical precedent for long-term success. Guarantees would have to be devised.

But it is not my opinion that counts here, but rather the feelings of the Arab militant...

MAHMOUD HUSSEIN: Until now, our dialogue has moved along in a kind of emotional void. There has been an intellectual tension between us, but feelings have not played a very big part. Now that we have reached the present, the moment in which we are living, and are talking about what will be happening during the coming months, it is important that you understand how very uncomfortable I feel.

We have begun to dig into living flesh now. The conversation touches on territories that are Arab, that are an inherent part of each Arab. Perhaps it is true that there are certain Arab leaders today who will be willing to give up a certain portion of this territory in the end. The Arab-Israeli negotiations are in the process of being transformed into a huge marketplace in which bits of territory are weighed against rockets and tons of oil. But I can tell you that for the Arab people this is a terribly painful thing, which they are tolerating only for the moment, because they hope, under the impetus of October, to finish with all this very quickly.

But the idea of bargaining with territories is not acceptable at all and would soon become unbearable if it became the subject of prolonged negotiations. The general feeling about the negotiations, which is still a bit vague, is that the Arab leaders are discussing ways of getting back the territories and not simply buying them back one by one in exchange for other things. I think I made it sufficiently clear yesterday that these territories are something very different from geographic spaces. They are the mainstays of sovereignty, of national dignity, and dignity cannot be cut up into pieces, it is not divisible. This can be seen in what President Assad said to Arnaud de Borchgrave, an editor at *Newsweek* who had remarked that the negotiations between Syria and Israel must have been very hard. The Syrian president said: "It is hard to argue with other people about our return to our own territory."

At present there is a gap between the bargaining that is going on at the higher levels and the completely different needs of the people. This ambiguity can persist for a while, but not indefinitely. If the Arab people begin to say to themselves that the Israelis are using the territories as trump cards, as a means of obtaining various concessions, they will begin to turn against the very principle of negotiation. The return of the territories is seen as a natural right, not as a favor from the Israelis.

SAUL FRIEDLÄNDER: One clarification. I said that from the very beginning Israel would promise to give back the territories by the end of the process. The initial promise would be given, then would come the successive stages of withdrawal. In my proposal, Israel would say from the very beginning: "You will have these territories, but only after five, or seven, or ten years, once the process has been completed and there has been a normalization of relations." So, from the very beginning there is this element which, as you say, is essential to the masses.

MAHMOUD HUSSEIN: Once the principle of the restoration of the territories has been acknowledged, unquestionably recognized by you, certain stages can probably be defined. Yet even in this case, time can't be toyed with. It is not a harmless factor. I will return to this in a moment.

We have just reached an understanding on an essential principle: the necessity for a return of the territories seen as restitution of a right. But precisely because this principle is essential, I am troubled to see that in the eyes of the Israelis, this does not apply to Jerusalem. It is as if we were preparing the way for the fifth Arab-Israeli War. You just spoke to me about the feeling of the Jews toward Jerusalem and other historic places. But what you say about the Jews also applies to the Arabs.

On this subject, everything is filled with emotion, and once again it is important to present the problem with all its emotional weight, so that people on the outside will not be tempted to shrug their shoulders about it. For us, emotion is politics at its greatest degree of intensity, it is the politics of a people who have not yet taken on a true identity, who are still facing the problem of being present or not being present in the world. The visceral quality, inseparable from their needs, comes from this. It is not at all irrational; it has all the rationality of questions of life and death.

You yourself recognize that if Jerusalem counts so much for the Jews, it counts just as much for the Moslems. And we should add the Christians as well. We can see from this that nothing can be done if the Jews give their feeling for Jerusalem more historical validity than the feelings of the Arab Moslems and Christians. The emotional dimension is essential, but on all sides. Within the walls of Jerusalem there are two rival emotional universes, and neither one has more right to survive than the other. When you say that Jerusalem is very important for you, this is understandable. But if this is translated into the statement, we must have Jerusalem all to ourselves, we will take it back from you—no. Jerusalem must be given to all those who find in it a part of their collective identity.

One last word about your proposal. The Arabs who speak for Jerusalem cannot be just any Arabs. They must be Palestinians, and no one else. This point wasn't made clear enough in your statement.

SAUL FRIEDLÄNDER: When I spoke of the Arab section, I purposely did not talk about whom it would be restored to because the whole of the Palestinian problem will be covered later in our debate. It is clear to me that it concerns either the Jordanians or the Palestinians, or Jordanians and Palestinians jointly, but it could be that it would concern only Palestinians. I did not want to talk about the Palestinians because I wanted to keep to the order of the discussion. It is entirely clear to me that the section to be given back could very easily become the capital of the Palestinian state.

MAHMOUD HUSSEIN: Yes, that is a good answer. As far as I am concerned, there is nothing ambiguous about it. The Palestinians are the ones who must consider the proposed solution, and then either accept it or reject it.

If the Voice of the People Could Be Heard...

JEAN LACOUTURE: I would like to put Mahmoud Hussein on the spot. Friedländer gave us a description of two "peace plans." One was an official plan and the other was his own approach to the problem.

It would be interesting to have this kind of double description from you as well. How would you, Mahmoud Hussein, as an Arab militant, describe the reaction of the Arab establishment to these two proposals—Mr. Rabin's* and Saul Friedländer's—and how would you describe your own reaction?

MAHMOUD HUSSEIN: This may be an exception, Saul Friedländer, but I would like to quote your current prime minister, Yitzhak Rabin, who stated a few weeks ago, again to Arnaud de Borchgrave: "Peace will not be made by the governments, but by the peoples." No doubt I am reading things into this image, but by putting it in this form, he nevertheless allowed a truth to emerge that went beyond what he was thinking. The agreements between the leaders will have no value other than the value the peoples give

*Yitzhak Rabin, chief of staff of the Israeli army during the Six Day War of June 1967, became head of the Israeli government in 1974.

them, and will endure only to the extent that the peoples accept one another.

This is why I will answer Jean Lacouture by saying that Mahmoud Hussein would probably find himself in agreement with Sadat and Assad about accepting Friedländer's proposals as a worthwhile basis for discussion. But these ideas can be accepted, or understood, in two different ways, depending on whether we are talking about right wing people or left wing people. Also, to carry it a bit further, they can be used in two different ways in Israel, by those who truly believe in them and by those who only want to use them to gain time to prepare for a confrontation under more favorable conditions. But let us return to the Arabs.

For the men in power these proposals are automatically translated into topographic maps, signed treaties, guarantees given by the major powers. In this context the way the people feel about each other is not taken into consideration. Traditional distrust, the distance between the cultures, the roots of past animosity, will not be eradicated. They will develop further, and find a nourishing soil in which to do so: in disputed areas or demilitarized territories; among mistreated populations, beginning with the Palestinians—who, even if they eventually obtain a mini-state, will feel hemmed in, constricted by many complications in the exercise of their sovereignty. In another connection, the system established for arbitrating the conflicts will allow the major powers to intervene continually, deciding between the parties, and this will certainly aggravate local feelings.

In the end, the leaders will set up a maze of crisscrossing, controlled borders, lined with barbed wire, and increasingly sophisticated arsenals buried in the desert around us. It will wind up being an immense Berlin Wall, which at best will permit certain commercial exchanges, certain contacts between businessmen, but it will nevertheless remain a Berlin Wall.

For Rabin, economic exchanges seem to mean the same thing as a reconciliation of the peoples, but not for me. Only under certain conditions can such exchanges lead to a real peace; in particular, the terms of the exchanges must be equal. Look at the February 1958 union of Egypt and Syria, and the delirious popular enthusiasm that followed it. Look at the beginnings of economic partnership that came out of this union. And then look at the results. After three years there were unbelievable animosities. Certain groups in Syria began to think that Egypt wanted to colonize them. Many Egyptians began to think that Syria was the cause of all their troubles. In September 1971, the divorce was consummated.

The eventual exchanges between Israel and certain Arab countries, assuming that they do take place one day, will never benefit in any way from the kind of spontaneous solidarity that brought Egypt and Syria together. The conclusion is self-evident: to hope that the reconciliation of the peoples will keep pace with increasing commercial exchanges is an illusion as old as capitalism itself.

Then, how would the Egyptian Left envisage the fulfillment of Friedländer's proposals? For the Left, the territorial divisions are necessary insofar as they correspond to fundamental aspirations— the right to national sovereignty of the various peoples. But these divisions do not even begin to resolve the problem. We are in complete agreement about the fact that emotions play a decisive role in these problems. But if emotions are at the origin of the conflict, they also form the basis for a solution. Serious declarations of intention, a certain spirit of reconciliation, even generosity, are infinitely more valuable than slide rules. If the Israelis, for example, declared that they recognized, without equivocation, without ulterior motives, and without subterfuge, the right of the Palestinian people to a sovereign national life, if they declared that each exiled Palestinian had the right to return to his country and that all questions concerning this issue should be resolved by an honest dialogue between Palestinians and Israelis, imagine the flood of emotion that would break forth all over the region!

At this stage, of course, all we can do is imagine it, for I see quite clearly that the men who are pulling the strings at Geneva are opposed to this kind of development. But that only shows the essential difference between the two approaches I am talking about. For me, the basic thing is that the peoples have confidence in one another, after so many years of having ignored or hated one another. And for the peoples to have confidence in one another, they must share the same feelings. Financial figures leave them cold; the balance of trade concerns them very little, or very indirectly in any case; contacts between businessmen from both sides will not bring them any closer together. What will bring them together is a sharing of a certain spirit, or the feeling of moving ahead in the same direction, or of fighting against common enemies. That is why we give notions like generosity and confidence such major importance.

JEAN LACOUTURE: Do you think, Mahmoud Hussein, that if suggestions similar to Friedländer's proposal were made at the opening of the Geneva conference by Yigal Allon*, head of the Israeli delegation, they would arouse interest among the Arabs?

MAHMOUD HUSSEIN: Naturally. And this brings us to the notion of time. Time is not an abstraction that can be easily grouped with other factors to form an equation that seems perfect on paper. It is a very concrete dimension of the situation. The Arabs are waiting for a solution, and living through this period with the feeling that the solution follows naturally from the October war, and that it will bring a natural end to the disputes with Israel. They are waiting for Israel to recognize their national rights in exchange for Arab recognition of Israel's existence—which they are now implicitly ready to give. It goes without saying that for them it is Israel that must make the first gestures of good will, because the Arabs are the ones who find themselves in the role of injured party. This is what the present period of waiting is all about.

But as time goes on, and more difficulties appear, and the hard line declarations from the Israeli leaders become more frequent, this patience will turn to impatience, and the Arabs will be tempted to think that they were wrong about Israeli intentions, that the changes expected after the October war will not come to pass, and that everything must be started all over again. The Arab peoples reason in terms of fundamental rights and not in terms of the balance of forces. In their eyes, the occupied territories are not

*One of the heads of the Israeli army in 1948, longtime vice premier, made foreign minister in 1974.

subject to dispute; they belong to them and are occupied. Each delay in giving them back changes the essential character of the Arab-Israeli solution. Instead of being a reciprocal recognition of rights, an elementary act of justice that can promote a reconciliation of basic attitudes, the negotiations are reduced to a kind of haggling that becomes more and more suspect.

Let us remember why the last war became necessary. It was supposed to enable the Arabs to regain their rights and at the same time prove to themselves that they were capable of holding their own in a fight against the Israelis. Now, though they have regained their self-confidence because of October, they have still not won the rights they fought for. They hope, they believe, that the one will follow from the other, that the territories will be given back, that the Israelis are making the connection between the two. But how much longer can they go on hoping? The war of attrition on the Golan Heights was the first bad sign. We began to feel that the Israelis were reluctant. All Arabs felt solidarity with the Syrians, and everyone began to wonder if the October war had really ended on October 24th. If, for example, the Israelis show a new intransigence over the question of Palestine, if they insist on the positions dating from 1948, if they challenge the extremely sensitive solidarity that all Arabs feel now with the Palestinians, the people's hope to see things resolved in depth, which rose with the impetus of the October war, will probably be destroyed. We will gradually begin to await another October, one to follow October 1973.

The pride that has been regained is as demanding as it is generous. The open-mindedness that crossing the canal made possible will disappear. Disappointment and bitterness will replace it; the increasingly somber impression will be that if we have not been able to solve this problem and move on to all the other problems, it is the fault of the Israelis, who have not understood anything, who do not want to understand anything. So whatever may result from the long sessions that will be launched at Geneva, the people will not benefit from it. Even if a solution finally emerges after a series of crises, of partial confrontations, of painfully extracted agreements, we will still only have a suspension of the state of war, and that will last only as long as the balance of

international and local forces lasts, since those forces will be the
basis for it. But the chance for a reconciliation of the peoples will
have been lost.

SAUL FRIEDLÄNDER: Again, I want to remind you that I don't agree
with you in always making this distinction between the masses and
the governments. It is perhaps helpful in certain situations. I don't
want to argue about it now, but we probably will have a chance to
talk about it again later.

You said that time is not an abstraction; I feel the same way. For
me, time is an absolutely concrete factor in this process. It is only
through this dimension that we can imagine a reconciliation of the
peoples. Reconciliation is not a formal term in my mind. You
noticed that I did not say that when the foreign ministers of both
parties had signed the treaty Israel would withdraw from the
territories. I made a clear distinction between the formal treaty and
the slow process of withdrawal by stages, which would be linked to
another series of measures already implying a certain underlying
reconciliation between the peoples. I mentioned the free movement
of people—and goods, of course—thinking that human contact and
joint enterprises necessarily implied permanent contact, constant
exchanges of views, which would give each side the feeling of
knowing the other better, as well as a certain reassurance about the
other's intentions. At that stage, the formal guarantees of security
which are so necessary at the beginning of the process will perhaps
be much less important.

In my mind, time is the crux of the whole affair; it should lead
from a formal settlement to a real settlement. The beginning of the
process is accompanied by a purely formal settlement, an agreement on how this promise of restitution can be carried out; the end
of the process is the actual restitution and the establishment of a
real peace.

But you should understand that in my remarks I am touching the
very limit of what an Israeli can say today—except for ideological
and political outsiders. I don't feel at all isolated, but I am really
very close to the edge of what is possible today and I ask you to
keep this in mind. If even this extreme limit is difficult for you to
accept, because of the speed with which you want to recover the

territories, then you should understand that there will be no one left
for you to talk to. It will not be easy to convince the majority of
Israelis that an idea like mine is viable. The common fear, in fact,
is that the Arabs will suddenly change their minds, and that they
will start up the war again at precisely the moment when all the
occupied territories, including the strategic points, will have been
returned.

As far as I am concerned, the relatively slow and gradual nature
of the process I am thinking of remains the only plausible answer,
the only answer which would eventually quiet these fears. Let us
try, then, to agree on a reasonable period, because an outright
rejection of these proposals would mean that, on the other side, you
will not find anyone to talk to.

MAHMOUD HUSSEIN: Wait a minute. To say that the Israelis will
give back this territory if...and another territory on the condition
that...can only have very negative effects in the Arab world. To
say that no one will want to talk with us if we do not accept your
premises is a kind of psychological blackmail. Our starting point is
not what is acceptable to Israel, but what is required by the Arabs.
If there is no possible meeting place between the two, we would be
tempted to say—too bad. It's unfortunate, but there's nothing to be
done about it. The Arabs can no longer accept the idea that what is
possible and not possible should be determined by Israel.

What we must do, then, is see how deep the gulf is that separates
us. We will probably come to the very bottom of this gulf. Things
are happening on both sides, possibilities are opening up, there is a
new willingness...and yet we have just seen that even the strongest
forces of reconciliation are thwarted by the forces of resistance that
history has created over the past fifty years, because they are rooted
in two separate universes that until now have been hermetically
sealed off from one another. If we stay where we are, if we don't
understand the enormous complexity of things and understand that
things have begun to happen, then it would be hard to see any
solution other than more wars.

The hope which I am formulating—and I am well aware how
tenuous it is—is that each side try to find a series of successive
balances, no matter how unstable or temporary, and that at each

stage these balances be based on a synthesis of the contradictory requirements of Arab dignity and Israeli security. In the months ahead, things must continue to move forward, even if only little by little, so that with each advance the Arabs will feel a little more certain of regaining their rights and the Israelis a litttle more certain of being accepted in the Middle East as a totally distinct community. Only in this way could some time pass without the people losing confidence in one another—not much time, because at each stage opposition to these measures will become more and more vehement.

The Arab peoples must come to feel that Israel's desire for security is not something that conflicts with their own desire for sovereignty. For my part, I think the moment of truth will come when the Palestinian problem is dealt with. And the moment for this is approaching. Everything will depend on how the Arabs feel you deal with this problem.

"Secure" Borders and "Recognized" Borders

JEAN LACOUTURE: Saul Friedländer, will people in Israel continue to make such a close connection between the basic question of security (the importance of which Mahmoud Hussein understands, as he has just shown) and the size of the controlled territories? We are living in a time of such highly sophisticated weapons that boundary lines would seem to be secondary. For a neutral observer like me, the problem would seem to boil down to one of recognition. A border can be "secure" only *because it is recognized*, because it is accepted by a neighbor who no longer harbors hostile intentions. Is it necessary to be neutral to think in this way? Aren't there people in Israel who think clearly enough to draw this kind of conclusion?

SAUL FRIEDLÄNDER: In a few sentences you have managed to sum up one of our most important debates; it has been going on since 1967, particularly since the war of 1973, and it involves those who are unconditionally in favor of security through the territories and those, like me, who think that security in the end depends on many other things and that the territories are only one element, which may become even less important as time goes on. And yet, knowing this, we still cannot completely discount the territorial factor in an area like the Middle East. Fortunately, we haven't yet

131

come to the point of fighting with missiles and nuclear bombs (when I say missiles, I mean long range ground-to-ground missiles and not antiaircraft or antitank missiles). It's still largely a matter of groups of men and mechanized weapons that must cover certain distances. In this context, you can't say categorically that the edges of the Golan Heights are no longer important, or that Sharm-el-Sheikh, for example, doesn't matter! These are strategic points in a conventional war. But perhaps the strategic element itself is not the most essential one.

The "territorialists" argument is more subtle than that—they want to deprive the Arabs of "temptations"... What if Sharm-el-Sheikh is given back and Egypt becomes hostile again; the easiest step, by holding Sharm-el-Sheikh, would be to close the Straits of Tiran. Or, what if the Golan Heights were given back to the Syrians? Wouldn't this be a temptation for them to begin firing on the kibbutzim in the Jordan Valley again? So it is not necessarily the strategic importance of these points in the war itself that is at stake, but their importance as possible trigger spots in new hostilities.

It could be that this is short-term thinking, but I don't completely underestimate it. That is why I feel we should accept a gradual process. As the atmosphere began to relax, we would give back the territories that are now seen as "temptations."

That is not all. It is important to put yourself in the other person's shoes. This is why I insist on the role of the time factor. Little by little Israel will grow used to seeing an Arab world that is somewhat appeased by the promise of eventually regaining the occupied territories. Relations will become closer and the importance of these strategic points will diminish. To paraphrase Golda Meir, we would say to ourselves: "Some of us have already shopped in Cairo," and therefore, "After all, Sharm-el-Sheikh is not so important." And yet, do not forget that Israel is taking a great risk in all this that should not be underestimated. This system has already been applied elsewhere, and it was not a success.

You will remember that this was pretty much the idea that the French had after the First World War. They had occupied the Rhineland and evacuated it by stages. There was supposed to be an evacuation of the three bridgeheads, Cologne, Koblenz, and Mainz at intervals of five years. In the end, the evacuation was much more rapid. But after a while, there was a resurgence of German nationalism, the Rhineland was remilitarized, etc.

JEAN LACOUTURE: I don't want to compete with you as a historian, but I don't think it is very generous to Yitzhak Rabin to compare him with Raymond Poincaré, who it seems to me provided us with some of the worst examples of diplomatic behavior. The occupation of the Rhineland and the reoccupation of the Ruhr played an important role in the rise of Nazism, in the frenetic rebirth of German nationalism. Goebbels is a product of this region and these circumstances. It would be a pity if an Arab Goebbels was born because the Israelis had stayed in the occupied territories too long!

SAUL FRIEDLÄNDER: That's a good point. I won't withdraw the comparison, but I should like to emphasize that there are ups and downs in history and that my plan is not a completely safe one. You can't say: "Friedländer, you are proposing an idea that might make trouble for you with your fellow Israelis, but after all, as far as Israel is concerned, it is really a way of playing it safe." No, it would involve taking certain risks and showing a certain faith in the future, and I think that this is what should be emphasized.

MAHMOUD HUSSEIN: One small point. If Israel holds onto Sharm-el-Sheikh or the Golan Heights, not only will there still be just as much temptation for the Arabs to attack Israel, but, as we saw with the October war, this temptation will become irresistible.

A Solution Imposed by Washington
and Moscow?

JEAN LACOUTURE: I have another question I would like to ask both of you. Could you each describe what we might call the politics of the superpowers, including the extent to which they share an overall goal and yet use antagonistic tactics. We would not be presenting the complete picture, and would not be entirely honest with ourselves if we did not take into account the considerable part played by the pressure, "advice," and general behavior of the two superpowers and the kind of solution they are devising.

SAUL FRIEDLÄNDER: Actually, I think that in any negotiation, this factor is essential, or even decisive, and as we know, the two superpowers are the ones organizing the Geneva Peace Conference. They are lavish with their "advice" to both sides.

I think that in the end they will agree on a formula, for better or worse for everyone. At the moment nothing is absolutely clear and I think if anyone is hanging back it is the Russians. We have been asking ourselves for quite a long time now if they have any stake in seeing a settlement reached. Some people think they do not, since as long as the tensions continue in the region, the Russians will penetrate further and further into the Arab world, taking advantage of the Arabs' need for military aid, and even economic and financial aid, to maintain and extend their influence there. Other people, including myself, believe that the global demands of détente—which is essential to the current Soviet leaders—will take precedence over regional interests, important as they may be. Therefore, the Russians are going to try to find a formula that compromises between the two, a solution that would give them prestige among the Arabs without breaking up the negotiations at Geneva. With this in mind, they will necessarily move in the direction of a political settlement, a settlement which will preserve détente, but will also go as far as possible toward satisfying the Arabs' political demands, so that they will appear to have defended the Arabs' interests better than anyone else. Since there is every reason to think that the Americans will adopt a policy that is less favorable to Israel than it was in the past, it seems likely that the two superpowers will little by little come to an agreement on a formula for preserving détente that they can both support, and that each will be prepared to make some concessions on a regional level.

What will this formula be? This takes me back to what I said earlier. It is quite possible that it would pose serious problems for Israel. It seems to me that the formula they are moving toward, step by step, perhaps inevitably, is quite similar to the 1969 Rogers Plan—in other words, the Arab version of the Security Council's Resolution 242 of November 1967, which calls for the restitution of *the occupied territories* and not just *occupied territories*. As I said, this position, which I think Washington will adopt, is going to cause the Israelis many problems. I was thinking of this when I brought up the possibility of a confrontation between Israeli policy and American policy. In the end, I think that only by offering the Americans flexible proposals like the one I described a short time ago, will we be able to find a way out of the impasse and avoid direct confrontation with them. Of course the Russians will make trouble for us. That is why I am once again speaking only of the Americans. That is also why I am trying to find formulas like the ones I proposed, in which time was the central factor.

The most important thing is that we must reach a compromise with the Arab countries; but we must also make suggestions to the Americans that are not too rigid, and do not get too far away from what their requirements will probably be, but which will at the same time provide a framework for negotiations, a situation in which Israel's security will not be threatened.

In any case, I am still convinced that if the Americans and the Russians tried to impose a formula for settlement on Israel that did not take into account the country's need for security, but rather demanded the *rapid* withdrawal from strategic areas, without complete normalization of relations with the Arab countries, Israel would say "no" and we would inevitably be headed for the kind of confrontation which I talked about this morning.

MAHMOUD HUSSEIN: Like you, I think the two superpowers are looking for a formula for the Middle East that they can agree on. I want to add that both of them would like to retain as many advantages as possible in the region, and keep some control over the course of events there. Concerning the problem of Palestine, for example, which hasn't really come up yet, it is clear that the USSR, which lost ground in Egypt and Syria, is trying to take charge of the formation of the State of Palestine, which could become a pro-Soviet platform and would be easy to manipulate because in itself it would be small, weak, and bounded on all sides by more or less pro-American forces. Moscow is obviously considering this prospect from the point of view of Soviet strategy and not from Palestine's national point of view.

It goes without saying that during all this, the Russians will be helping the Palestinians to make their voices heard by those who might prefer to drown them out, and the Palestinian leaders can hardly refuse to take advantage of this. But what we want to know is who will benefit more from this alliance in the end. The Russians obviously have ulterior motives for helping the Palestinians. Think of how scornfully they treated the Palestinian resistance only three or four years ago. Until very recently they refused even to refer to a Palestinian people. Their change of attitude is an extremely new thing. The Palestinians must take advantage of this while at the same time trying to retain as much autonomy as possible in relation to the Russians. As things are now, this will not be easy.

JEAN LACOUTURE: Do you think, Mahmoud Hussein, that the fact that both superpowers seem to be searching for a political settlement in the Middle East—in different ways, of course, but in ways that are probably converging—is reason to distrust them, particularly the Americans? Do you interpret this, as you interpret most of what America does all over the world, as being part of an imperialist plot that alienates you both intellectually and practically from this search for a political solution? Does the danger of finding yourself in the "same boat" as the Americans, in the course of this search, trouble you, and would it eventually cause you to refuse to join in?

MAHMOUD HUSSEIN: This is a difficult question. There is an extraordinary overlapping of interests here, and it is vitally important to understand what is going on if we want to distinguish between what is really in the people's interests and what seems to be in the people's interests but will actually result in further forms of dependence. The October 1973 war can lead to the resolution of the sharpest contradictions between the Israelis and the Arabs over the next few years. But even now it is producing new contradictions in the relations between the region and the superpowers, and in the long run these contradictions are just as serious from the people's point of view. Right now we are at a difficult crossroads, where the characteristics of the preceding stage overlap with the characteristics of the stage that is just beginning. This is the source of the complexity of a situation which has not yet fully formed.

We have already spoken of the fluidity of this situation, of the many possible combinations that could result from it. This is because of the fact that though the war was begun and directed by a very small number of people, it aroused the feelings of countless numbers of people, and shook the psychological structure that had governed the period from 1967 to 1973. So that it created a high level of energy throughout the whole region and inclined people generally to rethink the problem, and this is the most fertile thing about the present situation. This is why the leftist movements see new possibilities opening up for going beyond what they have ever done before.

A form of peace is being worked out at the top echelon, and the USA is already exercising a strong influence. But at the bottom echelons, there is another form of peace that does not have to be imposed right now, but can take root among the most open-minded people, both Israelis and Arabs, so that parallel movements can arise in opposition to the new form of American domination. However, mutual distrust is still very strong in the region, while popular approval of the United States, which many people consider the peacemaker of the region, is increasing again. We find ourselves in a paradoxical situation: The United States is the main force for bringing about an understanding between the leaders of the two camps, and consequently helping to free the people from the specter of continued war, at least for a while; yet at the same time it is posing the main threat, the threat of eventually entangling both camps in a network of military and economic agreements from which it will be more and more difficult for them to free themselves, a network of agreements which would only lead to an overarmed coexistence involving greater and greater risks of another confrontation if the international balance of power changes in the least.

It is therefore necessary, as we see it, to take advantage of this extremely equivocal period in which the United States is looming larger and larger but is not yet solidly established, and while things are still quite mobile both at the top and at the bottom, to make the Israeli and the Arab peoples, or at least the large numbers of leftists at their hearts, aware of the complexity of the situation, and to seize every possibility for reconciling them and preparing them for the *common* fight against the *common* enemy.

III

Third Day: The Future

questions—
arid land
that w
was

Do the Palestinians Exist?

JEAN LACOUTURE: We are going to start our third day of talks today by at last coming to grips with the Palestinian question, which has been constantly involved in our earlier debates, cropping up all the time, and which both of you characterized as central. I will first ask Mahmoud Hussein to talk about it and suggest what seem to him appropriate solutions.

MAHMOUD HUSSEIN: Yes, it is paradoxical that this question, which we all agree is the central question, has been left for the last day of our talks. But this paradox is in some way forced on us by the facts.

From 1948 to 1967 the great powers and the Israeli leaders simply tried to do away with the Palestinian problem, while most of the official Arab leaders were trying to take control of it and integrate it into their various strategies. During this whole time, the Palestinians had lost the ability to speak for themselves, to present their case in an independent way. Certain preparations had to be made, therefore, before they could be heard, and what I'm going to talk about today is basically what hopes and plans they began to express from the moment they regained their own identity. In other words, from 1967 on.

That was when we Egyptians realized that compared to the Machrek we were being somewhat reticent about these

about the Palestinians' profound roots in this strip of
which was also being claimed by the Israelis. It was then
e began to appreciate how intense the Palestinians' bitterness
over the fact that the Israelis had robbed them of their land. It
as then that we felt countless strong ties growing between us and
the Palestinians, who, instead of trying to end their suffering in a
spirit of blind revenge, were patiently trying to transform it in a
revolutionary way that would bring rebirth not only for them but for
all Arabs and even—ideally, at least—for the Jews who were
confronting them.

I am not going to try to give you a historical account of the
problem. But we must begin with what was the beginning of
everything, the indisputable fact that the Zionist *Yishuv*, the State
of Israel, was founded on robbery of the Palestinians. This is an
objective fact that is in no way contradicted, as we already said, by
the fact that the Jewish immigrants did not come to Palestine with
the intention of robbing the Palestinians of their land, but of
finding a homeland where they could be safe and far away from the
pogroms that had marked their history up to that point.

But the Palestinians were already there, and they were forced to
give up their place. Now some Israelis find consolation for this
unfortunate fact by reminding themselves that at one time, toward
the end of the First World War and during the twenties, the leaders
of the *Yishuv* tried to come to an agreement with the Arabs, and
that in any case they did not steal the first lots of land which they
cleared and cultivated, but bought them. Consequently, only the
Arabs were responsible for what happened after that. The increasingly brutal quarrels that broke out between the two communities
came about because of the stubbornness, or even the fanaticism, of
the Arabs, or at least of some of them. Peace was within their reach
and they let every chance for it escape them.

Anyone who talks this way is taking enormous liberties with the
historic truth. The Arab leaders who entered into dialogue with the
leaders of the *Yishuv* did not see how ambitious the Zionist plan
was, and certainly not what its long-term implications were. They
saw it only as the development of a Jewish community in Palestine,
within the larger Arab state which they thought would soon be
formed. The Balfour Declaration, which granted the Jews a na-

tional homeland, was drawn up in the vaguest terms just in order to encourage both Jewish hopes and Arab demands, which were in the long run contradictory.

We know very well what it represented from the very beginning for the leaders of the Zionist movement: the first step toward a Jewish state, in other words a separate territory, distinct from the area under Arab sovereignty and under the exclusive sovereignty of the Jewish pioneers. There is no doubt about that, because that was the basis of the Zionist enterprise—to create a country where the Jews would be at home and would no longer be a minority in another country.

Certainly this prospect was not acceptable to any Arab leader, whoever he might have been. Those who came into contact with the Zionist leaders at various times, starting with King Faisal,* did not grasp their underlying thoughts. At that time there was a very strong popular feeling in the whole of the Machrek in favor of the reunification of the entire region under one single Arab authority. The masses were basing their hopes on the action of their traditional leaders, Faisal most of all, who they felt was singled out to be king of the Machrek once it was liberated from the Turks.

But these leaders were not revolutionaries, to say the least! They were traditionalist, socially backward nationalists, and for them the restoration of Arab sovereignty did not imply the challenging of foreign supervision of the area. They were naturally ready to make agreements with the West because they felt it represented a civilization from which they had a great deal to learn.

On the individual level there were many landowners who had no objection, in principle, to selling part of their land to the Jews. They certainly didn't think this would lead to an exodus of the Palestinians; they simply saw it as a rather profitable transaction. But I must add that the Palestinian day laborers suffered from it right in the beginning, because more often than not they lost their means of livelihood and joined the swelling ranks of the unemployed. It is essential to realize that from this time on, the

---

*Oldest son of the Hashemite "Grand Sharif of Mecca," Hussein, he led the Arab Revolt of 1916. Proclaimed king of Syria in 1919, he was considered to be one of the leaders of the Arab world at that time. (He should not be confused with the recently assassinated king of Saudi Arabia.)

primary class contradictions between the landowners and the agricultural workers grew sharper, because their attitudes toward the
Yishuv were beginning to diverge. When the people running the
Jewish Agency dealt with the Palestinian landowners, they could
maintain that they were dealing with the Palestinians, pure and
simple, and that these differences were not their concern, but by
doing this they prevented themselves from seeing the reasons for
the revolts that were about to take place.

From the very first years on, the landowners had no qualms as
they pocketed the money from the sale of their lands to the Jewish
Agency, while the Palestinian laborers refused to leave these lands
and obliged the British troops to evict them *manu militari*. It should
be kept in mind that Arab society in Palestine was despotic and
traditionalist, that its political leaders were at the same time its big
landowners and its religious leaders, and that at that time they had
great influence over the Palestinian masses. Because of this they
could carry out numerous transactions which the masses did not
immediately protest in a purposeful and systematic manner, but
which created the ferment of a deep revolt, not only against the
Jewish Agency but also against the Arabs who were selling their
land, and most of all, it must be said, against the British army of
occupation, which was held to be responsible for all the people's
troubles.

> JEAN LACOUTURE: Your arguments about the feudal nature of
> the property sold to the Jewish Agency are striking. But can
> you really say that King Faisal was not committed to the Arab
> world at the beginning of the twenties? A case could be made
> for Faisal in 1920 being a sort of prefiguation of Nasser in
> 1956, given the historical evolution of the region. Just as the
> leaders of the FLN in 1960 were more or less the descendants
> of the Emir Abd al-Qadir of 1840. Didn't Faisal embody the
> collective aspirations of the Arabs at one time? However brief
> and conditional it might have been, the Faisal-Weizmann
> entente seems to have had a certain historic value. It makes us
> at least as uncertain about the authenticity and deep-
> rootedness of Zionism as did certain Marxist analyses just
> after the Second World War. One could say that when he

came into contact with the Zionist enterprise, Faisal revealed a troubling aspect of it.

MAHMOUD HUSSEIN: Certainly Faisal symbolized a great hope for the masses of the Machrek—precisely insofar as he identified with the national movement of that time—the plan to create a sovereign Arab kingdom, which the masses were hoping for. But Faisal's negotiations with Great Britain, and even more with the Zionist leaders, had nothing to do with the feelings of the people, who at that time were hardly involved in public life in the modern sense of the term—and who left their fate up to their traditional leaders. These transactions involved only the small group of Arab leaders. Their importance should therefore be judged not by how much they reflected any popular feelings, but by how much they showed Faisal's political awareness and the awareness of the leaders who surrounded him, and by how much the limits of their ability to master a very complex situation.

History was not slow to pass judgment. Faisal had placed all his hopes in England's promise of the kingdom he was praying for. This promise was not kept, because in the meantime London had agreed with Paris to divide up the region. So Faisal had been cheated. However, it was precisely at this point that he began collaborating with the Zionist movement—London, whom he still trusted, had advised him to do this, and it did not seem to endanger the creation of his kingdom.

The establishment of the Jewish homeland did not seem to him incompatible with Arab sovereignty because the kingdom he envisaged, in his traditional way, was perfectly open to non-Islamic enclaves of this kind, the rather protected enclaves that all Moslem states had contained in the past. Here we do indeed see a troubling aspect of Zionism, which did not make much effort to set Faisal straight, to explain to him that the Jewish homeland was gradually going to become an entirely sovereign state. It is therefore rather strange to take the dealings between Weizmann and Faisal as proof of the Zionists' initial good intentions. It is more a matter of sugarcoated bullets, as the Chinese would say.

Look at what happened when Faisal was swindled by the English. Did the Zionists even consider joining him against the

English? Of course not. The French and English project of dividing up the region and establishing a British mandate over Palestine was much more useful to them because it prepared the way for their ultimate goal. So, I think that we should let Faisal sleep in peace; we can't make him say anything very important, because he didn't do anything very important when he was alive.

SAUL FRIEDLÄNDER: I must say I didn't understand the drift of your question, Jean Lacouture. How did the Weizmann-Faisal meeting give Zionism a troubling aspect?

JEAN LACOUTURE: By troubling, I meant ambiguous. The episode actually shows that for some Arabs the Zionist enterprise was not purely colonial.

MAHMOUD HUSSEIN: For us, the ambiguity lies in the formulation of the long-range Zionist objectives. Which leads us to conclude that the period of collaboration between Arabs and Jews was quite brief, and also rather deceptive, since it was based on the ambiguity we are discussing. It certainly does not give anyone grounds for claiming that the Zionists did everything they could to avoid eventual confrontations.

Perhaps there were a number of Jewish pioneers, even certain leaders, who would have liked to avoid these confrontations, and who took various steps in that direction, but the antagonism was too strong between the Arab aspiration for sovereignty over the whole of the Machrek and the Jewish aspiration for sovereignty over one part of the Machrek, for these attempts to make much headway against the reality of the situation. The confrontation was the inevitable result of the Zionist project, and not of what has been called the "Arab refusal," a term which we do not like.

JEAN LACOUTURE: Since I am both Rodinson's friend and his editor, I would like to know why the term "Arab refusal" offends you.

MAHMOUD HUSSEIN: Rodinson had many things to say about this issue that were better put. For example, I can readily say how important I found his very fine piece called "Israël, fait colonial" [Israel: A Product of Colonialism] which opened the special June 1967 issue of *Les Temps Modernes*. But the title of the book he wrote afterwards, *Israel and the Arabs**, gives the annoying impression that there is an opposition between an established fact—Israel—and a sort of stubborn rejection of this fact by the Arabs. I would prefer the title to be "The Arabs and the Israeli Challenge," if you see what I mean. In any case, instead of "refusal," which has sterile, somewhat childish overtones, it might be better to speak of "resistance," which would give a better idea of the active, reclamatory nature of the refusal. But Rodinson is not on trial here.

To return to the relations between the Zionists and the Palestinian Arabs, it is possible that there actually was a historic occasion for collaboration which was not taken, but it did not come at the time or the place where we have been looking for it up to now. It was after the mass riots, after 1929. Another apparent paradox. The first forms of direct animosity between the two communities were beginning to crystallize then; it was precisely this fact that could have allowed certain Zionists, the most idealistic ones, the ones who had not been involved in the secret agreements with Great Britain, to see what large contradictions had been created by the leaders of the Zionist movement, and also to become aware of the social polarization which was beginning to appear within Palestinian society.

A truly popular rebellion was threatening to topple the traditional leaders; in 1935 with the al-Qasim hotbed of guerilla warfare, then in 1936 with the city strikes, and finally during the armed revolution of the countryside, this movement was producing local leaders among the people who had new ideas and were relatively free of the control of the traditionalist leaders—while these traditionalist leaders were trying to take back control of the movement by relying more and more on the weapon of chauvinism.

This is the unique historical occasion we are talking about! A wrenching—but profoundly revolutionary—revision could have

*The title of the original French edition of this book by Maxime Rodinson was *Israël et le Refus Arabe*, literally translated: Israel and the Arab Refusal. The book was published in English, however, under the title *Israel and the Arabs*.

inspired the most sincerely idealistic Zionists with the idea of basic
solidarity with the Palestinian guerillas against the British army.
Apparently this is not a purely abstract notion either. Certain
pioneers considered it. The Communists of that time did too. But
they remained marginal figures. As a whole, the *Yishuv* sided with
the English once again. But this time it no longer had any excuse.
It was confronting the Palestinian people, the most disinherited
segments of it, the most revolutionary groups within it.

SAUL FRIEDLÄNDER: I don't want to interrupt your account, and in a
moment I will answer at greater length, but all the same, one
question to clarify what you are saying: Could you name just one
popular Arab leader who would have been prepared, at the time of
the Arab revolt in 1936, to join the Jewish settlers in a sort of
united front against the British? I myself can't think of any. That
does not basically affect your analysis, but if you had some
concrete examples to give it would perhaps help.

MAHMOUD HUSSEIN: Even if leaders like that did exist, their names
would have been shrouded in silence not only by the English or by
the Zionists, but also by the Arabs in power, who were dismayed to
see these insurgent leaders rising up from the towns and villages
(during the period between 1936 and 1939) and defying their
political authority. But let us say right away that we don't think
there were popular leaders at that time who would have considered
collaborating with the Zionists, seeing what the Zionists were
doing.

The embryo of an exclusively Jewish state was already embodied
in the Zionists' policy of employing strictly Jewish labor in the
Jewish fields and factories. This autarkic society was in the process
of carving out an economic area from which the Arabs were totally
excluded, and this affected the Arabs in two ways: economically,
because they had less and less work; and what was worse,
ideologically, because they could not tolerate the idea that a part of
their historic patrimony—which was sacred, we must remember—
could be formally torn away from the Arab-Islamic community.

The kind of collaboration we have just described means, seen in
context, that some of the Jewish pioneers, realizing what frustra-

tion the Zionist policy had caused, would dissociate themselves unequivocally from the rest of the *Yishuv* and ally themselves with the Palestinian revolutionaries against the English and against the other Zionists, in order to create a truly democratic and multinational Palestine, abandoning once and for all the idea of exclusive Jewish sovereignty over any part of the territory.

In other words, this implies that the first step toward fraternizing between Arabs and Jews would be taken by the Jews and not by the Arabs—by those Jews who had understood the terrible harm they were causing the Arabs. Without such a step, it is not easy to see what could have made the revolutionary Palestine leaders approach the Jews, who were driving them out of their homeland.

Between the two wars, the leaders of the *Yishuv* were establishing the institutions of the future state according to a plan which they knew would be unacceptable to the Arabs in the long run. This is why it was logical for them not to seek an alliance with the Arab national movement but rather to profit from its weaknesses and take advantage of the incoherence of its leaders and the fragility of its popular organizations to establish themselves as solidly as possible, at the expense of the movement.

One general conclusion about this period, in which so many things happened whose effects we are still feeling today. Contrary to what people think, until the approach of the Second World War there was no serious tension between the mandate power and the *Yishuv*. The British army and British diplomacy protected the Zionist enterprise against the growing Arab revolt, and only when this revolt grew to an unexpected height and many Arab heads of state who were customers of England's—Egypt, Saudi Arabia, Iran—became worried about it, did London begin to change its policy. But earlier England had done the *Yishuv* an unfortunate favor. It had cleared the ground for it by crushing the first nation-wide Palestinian popular movement. It should not be in the least surprising that a deep well of bitterness has accumulated over the years since then and will take many years to evaporate.

SAUL FRIEDLÄNDER: I think you are simplifying many things.

First of all, during the period we are talking about, contacts took place between the most representative elements within the *Yishuv* and what seem to me the most representative elements within the Palestinian groups—aside from fanatics like Hajj Amin el-Husseini—namely between Ben-Gurion and Mussa Alami. I don't know if you are familiar with these conversations. Both sides tried to see a way for the two peoples to come to an understanding. It unfortunately ended in nothing, but it still provided the opportunity for long discussions, the record of which Ben-Gurion himself published a few years ago. So the facts are much more complex than you imply.

Secondly, you must be aware that within the *Yishuv* there was a small but prestigious group fighting for a binational, Judeo-Palestinian or Palestinian-Jewish State. The prominent figures in it were people like Buber, Ruppin and later Magnes, who was president of the Hebrew University. This proposal for a multinational state met with total rejection by the Arabs. In fact only one Arab was in favor of it then—his name escapes me at the moment—and he was assassinated.

A third remark occurs to me. You say, "Why didn't the Jews ally themselves at that time with the Arabs who were fighting against the English?" Well! Things just don't work that way! First, you would be hard put to find just one Arab among those who were fighting the English who would have been prepared to act in a similar way or who would have responded positively to any Jewish initiative at that moment. But the Arab revolt was not directed against the English! It was primarily directed against the "Zionist implantation" which the English had to protect. It is clear that the Jews were collaborating militarily with the English in order to defend themselves against the attacks of Husseini's groups and others during the years between 1936 and 1939.

I toss the ball back to you by asking a similar question. Why didn't the Arabs, during the years immediately following, the period from 1939 to 1945, join the Jews in a united front, after the immense catastrophe which had descended on them in Europe and which obliged them to try to impose their will on the English in Palestine—in other words, make the British open the doors of Palestine to immigration. The lack of solidarity with which you reproach the Jews during the years 1936 to 1939 was even more striking on the part of the Arabs during the period from 1939 to

1945. I suggest that we not follow the meanderings of history but concentrate on what is essential.

MAHMOUD HUSSEIN: We are not trying to write a history book, but even so, there are some larger and quite helpful truths to be found in the maze of smaller details, if we want to understand the present problem in depth.

How could you expect the Palestinians to consider fraternizing with the Jews just after their revolutionary movement had been crushed by the English army and the groups of armed Zionists that were helping them? Besides, that episode was only the culmination of a period in which the Palestinian peasant had regarded the Zionist settler as a stranger who had come with the protection of the English soldiers to chase him off the land he was cultivating and take his place.

SAUL FRIEDLÄNDER: Once again, I think you are presenting a distorted view of those years. It is possible that from an objective point of view the Palestinian peasant could be seen as being robbed. I am not sure he saw the situation in that light. He was hostile to Jewish settlement, but we don't really know what his point of view was.

On the other hand, you said, "The Jews came to drive away the Palestinian peasants," and here I can assure you—you can check up on this, at any point in the history of that period—that the intention of the Jews at that moment was not in any way to drive out the Palestinians. You may tell me that this is naive, and that objectively it doesn't change anything. Subjectively, the intention—admittedly naive—was to live side by side with the Palestinians. You have to admit this about the Jewish pioneers of that time: they certainly had a way of looking at things which we would consider naive today. They thought they would arrive in Palestine and be accepted because they were bringing a technical civilization that would benefit everyone who lived in the region. Objectively, the situation was different, and here I will use an almost Marxist method of analysis in emphasizing the difference between subjective will and objective reality. But it must be said, in order to reestablish the historic truth—insofar as we can speak of truth—that the Zionists had a well-defined subjective will, but that the objective results of their action did not tally with their primary intention.

MAHMOUD HUSSEIN: One more remark. You said, "The peasant was against Jewish settlement." No. He was against the robbery which it involved on an increasingly large scale within the framework of the plan for a national homeland. Before the Balfour Declaration the presence of the Jewish colonies did not give rise to a Palestinian revolt. You say that the intention of the Jewish immigrants was to live side by side with the Arabs. Be that as it may. That was completely plausible until the First World War, before the Balfour Declaration. But afterwards? When the Arabs, in greater and greater numbers and more and more unequivocally, refused to play along, and when they revolted against the Zionist plan, how did the Jewish pioneers react?

There is an impasse here from which the Israelis cannot extricate themselves in retrospect by simply saying: "In the beginning, we didn't know there were people in Palestine." Yet this is constantly asserted to this very day, even by pacifists like Uri Avnery. How did those Arabs, whom they wanted to live side by side with, suddenly evaporate? It is really difficult to believe that the Zionist leaders are being honest about this.

One can very easily believe that the little people, the relatively ignorant artisans and workers who came from Eastern Europe in the simple hope of regaining the land of their ancestors, were not very aware, in the beginning, of whether or not there was a Palestinian population.

But certainly the Zionist leaders must have known that there was one. There was a great deal of uncultivated land and a very sparse population of peasants, but they were certainly visible. There were also Palestinian towns, which were not inhabited by ghosts and which some of the Zionist leaders visited before 1914! And finally the Jewish settlers who established themselves around the turn of the century were familiar with life in Palestine, and had contacts with the Arab community which were entirely real and which were studied by the early leaders of the Zionist movement. They cannot therefore plead ignorance and lack of culture as extenuating circumstances.

From Innocence to Zionism

JEAN LACOUTURE: "A land without men for men without a land." Doesn't this famous phrase sum up a whole period of Zionist consciousness?

SAUL FRIEDLÄNDER: If memory serves me correctly, this phrase was first used before the First World War. In fact, this was the vision of the very first Zionists, who had no notion of Palestinian reality, since, as you can well imagine, this reality was hardly tangible for Europeans arriving in Palestine. The country was not densely populated and was quite undeveloped before the First World War. I don't think that the Arabs would even want to deny this. Beyond this, let's be fair to the Zionists of the twenties and thirties. They knew that there were Arabs in Jaffa, Haifa, and of course in Jerusalem. But their idea, especially during the twenties, was that they could live peacefully side by side with these Arabs, without depriving them of anything. Perhaps this was naive of them, but even so, this is the way they saw things. They said to themselves: "We are bringing in modern technology, developing agriculture, making development possible for the people who live here, and we will move forward together."

It is true that they advocated "Jewish work on Jewish soil" as the basic slogan of the return of the Jews to the land. It was not a matter of taking anything from the Arabs, but of giving the Jew a new dignity. The Jew would no longer be a merchant or an intellectual, but he would work the land, which did not exclude the possibility that the Arabs would be working their own land, alongside the Jews. We must try to understand how Zionists of the period saw things. It was Weizmann who said in 1923: "We must reach an agreement with these people (the Arabs) who are so close to us and with whom we lived in harmony in the past." A year later Ben-Gurion wrote: "History commands us to live with the Arabs, and you cannot tamper with what history commands."

Tensions between the two communities worsened after the Arab attacks in 1929, then even more with the Arab revolt in 1936. It was then that the *Yishuv* understood that Arab hostility was absolute and decided to act accordingly. It was then that a man like Ruppin, who had founded the "Brit Shalom" movement (Alliance for Peace) and who was in favor of a binational state, began to despair over the possibility of an agreement. But you know that even during the war of independence in the spring of 1948, Jewish leaders such as Shabtai Levi, the mayor of Haifa, tried to convince the Arabs of the region not to leave and to continue to live beside the Jews.

MAHMOUD HUSSEIN: As the Zionist pioneers began to understand the Arab hostility toward their enterprise, how did they act? Did this lead them to question the validity of the enterprise? Not at all. It led them to fight the Arabs even more violently. The conclusion that we can readily agree upon is the following: Whatever the good will or honesty of the Zionists toward the Arabs during a certain period, it did not count very heavily in regard to their determination to achieve their goal, whether or not the Arabs wanted it. And this is the heart of the problem.

Objectively speaking, the Zionist project implied despoiling the Palestinians, even if this was not a conscious motive on the part of the immigrants, at least in the beginning. But let us try now to go a little deeper into this objective/subjective opposition that you brought up. I find your remarks very similar to an idea I used five years ago in my book *Class Conflict in Egypt*: subjectively, the pioneers were imbued with an ideal; objectively, they became the oppressors of the Palestinian Arabs. In the analysis of the Zionist phenomenon this opposition is operative and useful on a certain level; but it is somewhat superficial and mechanical. The good faith with which the Zionist pioneers despoiled the Palestinians must itself have been flawed; the idealism was tainted from the beginning. Thus this opposition between objectivity and subjectivity—which is too schematic—does not take into account the astonishing persistence of Zionist naiveté, the conviction that they were in the right, which was maintained against all odds, in spite of the realities that confronted them.

I don't at all want to do away with this notion of naiveté; I think that it is even essential for understanding Zionism. I simply want to give it its true place, its historical content. I said that I do not for a moment think that this naiveté is an excuse for ignorance of the facts. Weizmann had lengthy discussions with the British ministers; their conversations were not at all poetical—they were based on maps, figures, and reports. As for the immigrants who left for Palestine without knowing what they were getting into: a few weeks, at most a few months, would have been enough to convince them of the presence of the Arabs—and their resistance. And yet most of them were sincere idealists. What are we to make of this?

What was the flaw in this idealism, what was the worm in the apple? It was the ideology of Western colonialism, the general atmosphere of European society, and therefore of the Jewish communities in the West, the idea that the Eastern civilizations were somehow backward. In the East—that vague universe inhabited by men of color—the European sincerely believed that he would be welcome because he was the bearer of modern civilization. That some areas of the East were less populated or more populated than others was not really important. That was an alibi of secondary importance. The Eastern populations could only profit by a European presence among them.

The civilizing mission which Europe felt itself to be invested with over the course of the last two or three centuries was used to justify all sorts of crimes. When Europe conducted colonial expeditions and wars, when it displaced entire populations and even sometimes annihilated them, when it increased the exploitation of their national resources, when it sapped all the productive energies of several generations of men and women, Europe acted with the utmost naiveté, saying that this was the price that had to be paid for exporting civilization to the rest of the world.

To give an example specifically related to Zionism—the pioneers of the New World, the emigrants from England, Germany, and Sweden, who had all been more or less persecuted in their own countries, embarked for America filled with good Christian motives, armed with an idealism of the same kind as the Zionist pioneers in Palestine. They thought, naively, that the American Indians would gladly welcome them; and if violence ensued, it was only in self-defense, for the Indians, who had understood nothing, didn't want to let matters rest.

Let us conclude. The naiveté of the Zionists between the two world wars was very real, but it was not innocent, for it bore the ideological stamp of nineteenth century European conquests. The strong socialist ideals of the first generations of pioneers certainly influenced the egalitarian and fraternal relationships in the *Yishuv*; but this idealism also bore the seeds of racism, which it shared with other European nationalist movements—the ideological malformation which posited that white men were superior to other people, that their rights were more real than the rights of others, that they counted for more.

That is why the Zionist pioneers, even when they recognized the importance of the Arab population and understood the intensity of its resistance to them, continued to believe in their own rightness and to fight against the Arabs while saying that this was not what they had wanted to happen. This explains why there was no development of mass consciousness in the *Yishuv*, no major split of a part of the pioneer society in revolt against the original Zionist project.

SAUL FRIEDLÄNDER: To a certain extent, I think this split did take place. But because of the circumstances, it was then reabsorbed. In my previous remarks I pointed to the existence of a group that conceived of no other possibility than the binational solution—who believed that Jews and Arabs must share a common fate in Palestine. I mentioned Buber's group, but in fact the advocates of this approach included a more important political group, the whole left wing of the Zionist movement, the *Hashomer Hatzair* (Young

Watchman), whose members were in favor of the creation of a binational state. On the Arab side, however, this met with total rejection. There was no Arab willing to see things in this way. Obviously, the weight of events in the Western world, the acceleration of history in Europe and then in the Middle East during and immediately after the Second World War, pushed this group to the side. But they had agitated as much as possible for this idea, and it was only in 1947–48 that they lined up with the majority position, which was for an exclusively Jewish state and whose best known supporter was Ben-Gurion.

This whole process was far more complex than what I have just described, and the split that you were talking about, retrospectively, did take place at a certain moment. There were violent disputes within the Zionist movement, precisely about this question of goals; then history speeded up the evolution of one group and forced the others to abandon their position because there had been no real reaction from the Arabs.

MAHMOUD HUSSEIN: I think I have explained why the idea of a binational state was not acceptable to most Arabs at that time, because it seemed to imply permanently giving up the hope of Arab sovereignty over a part of Palestine.

I would like to add something to a point you raised concerning the possible development of a movement of solidarity between Palestinians and Jews during the years 1939 to 1945. I said that after the repression of 1936–1939 this was not conceivable, but it is important to mention also that the Palestinians, as well as most of the other Arab countries, felt no sympathy at all for the cause of the Allies during the first years of the war. Their hereditary enemies, their direct oppressors, were the English and not the Germans—who, in fact, were looked on with favor, because few people understood what the Nazi regime really represented. It was only when the Russians entered the war that the sympathies of the Arab people turned toward the Allies—but this was because of the Soviet Union and had nothing to do with the English.

JEAN LACOUTURE: There is an aspect of your conversation that struck me as quite surprising. Are you admitting, Saul

Friedländer, that resistance against the English was more
intense on the part of the Arabs than on the part of Jewish
organizations? Personally, my argument for the legitimacy of
the State of Israel is largely based on this resistance to a
colonial force. It is this struggle for liberation, rather than the
struggle of Judah Maccabee, that justifies Israel's existence in
my mind.

Am I wrong in overestimating this aspect of the problem?

MAHMOUD HUSSEIN: The interest of our exchange of views on the
period between the two wars is to show that during this period there
was an obvious alliance between the English and the Zionists, and
that the resistance to the British was carried on essentially by the
Palestinians. There was some friction between the representatives
of the Crown and the *Yishuv* and these differences undoubtedly
became quite important at the time of the White Paper, but they did
not really challenge the system of alliance that characterized this
period. Until 1938, for example, there was collaboration between
the British troops and Zionist organizations. It was during this
phase that the unbridgeable gap developed between Jews and Arabs
on Palestinian soil.

SAUL FRIEDLÄNDER: Here I am in total disagreement with your
analysis. I think that if Zionism could not completely detach itself
from Great Britain before the end of the Second World War, it was
not because it sought out this situation, but because it was being
confronted with Arab resistance at a moment when Great Britain
was in a position to help, and because there was no other possible
recourse.

Nevertheless, as soon as Great Britain began to demonstrate real
opposition to the Zionist project, especially after 1939, with the
publication of Chamberlain's White Paper, the Jews of Palestine
found themselves faced with a grave dilemma, because at that same
moment the war in Europe was beginning. Was it better to stay with
the English against the Nazis, or, in spite of everything, to fight the
English because of the White Paper? You know the famous phrase
of Ben-Gurion, "To be for the English as if there had been no White
Paper, to be against the White Paper policy as if there had been no

Hitler''; that is to say, to reconcile these two attitudes, which
would not please everyone. . .Two resistance groups developed to
continue the struggle against the English during the Second World
War—the Irgun and the Stern group. But, you can't call them the
natural allies of the Arabs, because those who continued the fight
against the English were Jewish nationalists of the furthest
extreme, and they were also the most hostile to the Arabs.

MAHMOUD HUSSEIN: We do not disagree over the fact that there
were problems between the British and the Zionists after the former
created serious obstacles for Jewish immigration, even though these
problems did not really degenerate into outright antagonism until
after the Second World War. It was natural that from then on the
Zionists would be opposed to England. But what I find very
important, very significant in what you have just said, is the
Zionists' attitude during this period toward the English; it is
identical to the Israelis' attitude in 1974 toward the United States,
as you described it yesterday.

You say, in effect, that the Zionists sided with the English
because the British army was fighting the Arab guerillas—and one
must assume that there were reasons for this, that there were
common interests between England and the *Yishuv* that justified
this military action—and then you say: "As soon as the English
changed their attitude, we turned against them." That is exactly
what you said when you were speaking about the United States.
You were happy when they were helping you against the Arabs, but
as soon as they begin to exert pressure against your strategy, you
resist them.

This is the basic difference between your attitudes toward the
great powers, toward foreign presence in the region, and our
attitudes. For you, in the beginning, there is complicity with one of
the powers, and it is only when problems arise that you oppose
them. There is complicity because, from its very origins, the
Zionist project was against the movement of Arab liberation and
only the enemies of this movement could protect you against it; and
there is complicity because on the economic level you depend very
heavily on aid from the West to live as you do.

With us, on the contrary, there is a spontaneous rejection of all outside interference. This feeling is more or less conscious, more or less violent, according to the social classes and the periods of our history that are involved, but it is a deep and continuous feeling and it underlies the successive advances of the Arab national movement. Foreign "protectorship" has been imposed by force, for periods of varying length, but the general attitude toward it has always been one of rejection, and this rejection has been so tenacious, so deeply rooted in the substratum of history, that even the most timid leaders, even the most conservative social classes, have had to take it into account. With us, "guardianship" of this kind has always been synonymous with repression, cultural domination, and exploitation. There is no possibility that it would one day be accepted by the Arab peoples.

SAUL FRIEDLÄNDER: I understand your reasoning perfectly, but, as I told you at the beginning, I do not share your general terms of reference. Obviously, for a liberal Zionist like me, the essential thing is a rational and human realization of the Zionist dream— later we will speak of all the positive aspects of this term. As a result, for me the main problem remains the opposition facing this project, and I can only be glad of any aid that is given, even if it comes from the outside, and I can only fight against outside opposition. Under the present circumstances, I don't think of a struggle against an ally, even a temporary one, in the general terms of a struggle against imperialism, since, personally, I don't accept that general frame of reference.

MAHMOUD HUSSEIN: We are not concerned here with an opposition between two visions of the future—yours and mine. We are concerned with a very real opposition, past and present, between two logical systems: that of the society founded by the Zionists, which is dependent on Western capitalism, and that of Arab society, which developed a movement to struggle against Western capitalism—not so much because it was capitalist, but because it oppressed the Arab people. Independently of all value judgments, this shows us how great the gap is that separates us.

But let's get back to the specific problem of the Palestinians. After the Second World War, the die was cast.

When the State of Israel was proclaimed, the war that broke out against it was a regular war, led by the conservative Arab states. The Palestinian people, still demoralized by the defeat of the 1936–39 revolutionary movement, which had wiped out most of its revolutionary cadres, could oppose the Zionists only in an isolated and hopeless way—for the Arab states, far from having supported the movement, had helped to crush it.

I won't lay stress on the war itself, and on the things that Israel gained because of the Arab defeat. These are well known facts. The essential thing to remember is the immense frustration that was felt in the Arab world.

The only Arab state which really profited from the war was King Abdullah's Jordan. He obtained a rather vague kind of guardianship over the left bank of the Jordan and then annexed this area *de facto* to Transjordan and thus created the kingdom of Jordan. He then became an objective accomplice of Israel in a joint effort to make Palestine disappear from the map, to make the world forget that a Palestinian people existed. Since then, officially, there are only Israeli Arabs, Jordanians from the left bank, and the UNRWA refugees.

I should quickly add that King Abdullah and his present successor, King Hussein, are not the only ones to blame. Even if the other Arab leaders continued to swear that they would avenge the Palestinians, they were all participating, to greater or lesser degrees, in a gigantic enterprise of demoralizing these same Palestinians—preventing the Palestinians from organizing and contributing to division through their own subtle maneuvers. Each Arab leader tried to create a following among the Palestinians favorable to his own stategy. This was the most horrible period of Palestinian history—a period of exile, dispersion, and humiliation, a period when a people begins to have doubts about itself. To use a term that you are quite familiar with, it was a period of diaspora.

There is no doubt that during this period exile was considered something temporary by the Palestinians. The State of Israel was an aberration. In the real sense of the word, it was unbelievable. Palestine, on the other hand, was still a palpable reality; it was particular neighborhoods, villages, houses, which each person had engraved in his memory and which the daily reality of the refugee camps only purified from year to year. It is important to emphasize the Palestinians' view of Israel during this period. Israel was a foreign body in their universe, which only a few years before not only did not exist, but was not even imaginable. All the Arab leaders, Palestinians or not, endlessly repeated to them that there was not the slightest question of giving anything to the Zionists, not even an inch of territory.

So everything that has happened since 1948 can only have appeared as a nightmare to them; sooner or later, they felt, they would wake up and find themselves in their own country, as before.

It was after the Suez aggression in 1956 that a true current of resistance developed among Palestinian youth. The Israeli army took over the Gaza Strip, which was at that time under Egyptian control—and the people there found themselves alone, without weapons, face to face with the occupier. The difficulties that they experienced during this period of several months in organizing themselves to carry out acts of sabotage, convinced them of the importance of establishing Palestinian organizations for combat, independent of the armed forces of the other Arab states.

The founders of al-Fatah were all the more prompted to create these organizations because the withdrawal of the Israeli forces in early 1957 was accompanied by the arrival of UN forces—which were supposed to maintain the status quo on the Egyptian-Israeli borders. The aim of al-Fatah became that of preparing Palestinian youth to take autonomous military actions, so as to undermine a status quo which froze the Palestinian question and to gradually create conditions favorable to the participation of the principal Arab armies in a Palestinian war of liberation.

In 1967 these aims were achieved, but the result of the confrontation was very different from what had been hoped for. On the one hand, the Arab armies were defeated; on the other hand, for a period of two or three years, the Palestinians found themselves once again in the forefront of things and bore an overwhelming responsibility in terms of the rest of the Arab world—that of bearing witness, not only to the rebirth of the Palestinian personality, but at the same time to the aspiration of all Arab peoples to wipe out the disgrace of the June war, to take up the challenge once again of the new Israeli power, and to prepare for a new war of liberation.

This is the role they assumed between 1967 and 1970 with the series of commando operations that were undertaken in the occupied territories. The newspapers all over the world talked enough about these operations at the time to make it unnecessary to do so now. But what the newspapers were not able to show was the enormous importance of these operations for the Arab people—the pride, the joy that the fedayeen were able to inspire after the confusion of the June defeat, and the subversive nature of this pride in the various Arab states. Because, as it renewed the self-confidence of the peoples, it drove them to protest against the immobility and indecision of their leaders; it helped sap the moral authority of the regimes in power, and it began to upset the Arab ruling circle more and more. This is what allowed the king of Jordan to prepare and carry out the massacres of September 1970, taking advantage of the embarrassed silence of some leaders and the complicity of others.

If the voice of the fedayeen has begun to quiet down since then, it is less from Israeli pressure than from the repression of the Arab governments, which did not forgive them for having drowned out their own voice—for a time even Nasser's star seemed to fade.

In the space of three years all the autonomous bases of resistance in Jordan, Lebanon, and Syria have been dismantled. The Palestinians have met with more and more difficult problems; they have become increasingly dependent on the Arab governments, which have been trying to retake the initiative and which want no part of the PLO* unless it goes along with their strategy.

However, the most advanced currents of Arab opinion, which are powerless to change this orientation, make every effort to stand in solidarity with the Palestinians, notably, in Egypt and Lebanon, by means of massive demonstrations against their governments, by answering the needs of the resistance, by recognizing its right to use all possible means to defend itself.

In all this there is a confused feeling of gratitude on the part of the Arabs toward the Palestinians, a moral debt with very deep roots, no doubt combining in an obscure way a guilt complex for the years between 1948 and 1967—during which the Palestinians were abandoned—and thankfulness for the years between 1967 and

*Palestine Liberation Organization headed by Yasir Arafat.

1970, during which they alone, immediately following the defeat, raised the flag of Arab pride.

This feeling is rarely formulated in this way, but it often shows itself in an indirect manner. For example, since the Egyptians and then the Syrians began negotiating with Israel, there has been a certain disquiet expressed by the people of the two countries. People are wondering whether the leaders are in the process of solving their own problems by sacrificing the Palestinians; they wonder whether it was necessary to separate the Egyptian and Syrian questions from the Palestinian question. People tend then to support the fedayeen in everything they are trying to do, not because they go along with each of their actions, but because they fear that the Palestinians might be abandoned by the Arab ruling circles; consequently, the people recognize their right to express themselves by any means... If these fears were definitely confirmed, the Arab people would reject all agreements with Israel, no matter how advantageous they might be for Egypt or Syria.

SAUL FRIEDLÄNDER: What you are saying is that without a solution to the Palestinian problem there will be no solution to the Israeli-Arab conflict, that the Palestinian problem in some way expresses the essence of the conflict. I am going to surprise you—this is also my opinion. I will go even further. In spite of all the official statements, I think that this is the unspoken feeling of the average Israeli. But understand me well. One can say for example—and many people say it in Israel—that the attitude of the Palestinians toward Israel represents the real attitude of all the Arabs, without any of the hypocrisy. One can also say—and again many people say it in Israel—that the rest of the Arabs would use the same methods as the Palestinians if they could. In the assassinations committed by Palestinians over the past few years, particularly at Kiryat Shemona and Maalot, there is something so repugnant, so horrible to the Israelis that if the Palestinians continued to do such things and if they seemed to be representative of the true Arab feelings toward the Israelis, there would no longer be any possibility of an agreement of any kind, either with the Palestinians or with the other Arabs. Israel will never talk with terrorist organizations, but neither will it talk with Arab governments that consider terrorism a legitimate form of confrontation.

In short, I believe as you do that we cannot separate the conflict as a whole from the Palestinian question, but I would like to say to the Palestinians, and to the other Arabs as well, speaking as one Israeli among many others, that considering the Palestinians representative of all the Arabs can create many problems in its own right. The Palestinians should know where terrorism can lead them—they should know it and the whole of the Arab world should know it with them.

MAHMOUD HUSSEIN: We must consider the question of Palestinian representativeness on two levels. First, they speak on behalf of a certain number of national demands, which all the Arab peoples are in favor of; second, they speak for themselves, deal with the specific problems they must face as Palestinians.

As I mentioned before, there is a gap between the situation of the Egyptians or Syrians, for example, and the situation of the Palestinians. The former are not threatened in their national life; they have obvious aspirations in regard to Israel, but they express them from a position of historical stability and national continuity which nothing has essentially challenged. The Palestinians have not yet reached this point. Their collective existence is officially denied by Israel. This is another anguish that they feel much more strongly than the Arabs around them. It is as if the future of each one of them were being discussed and rediscussed by other people. It is an unbearable situation, which makes for different sorts of reactions among the Palestinians.

For the majority of them, it is a question of anxious waiting, lived through with greater or lesser difficulty depending on whether they are on the West Bank, in Transjordan, Lebanon, or Syria. The members of the resistance movement, as for them, oscillate between two principal tendencies: one attitude which leads them to hope for an honorably negotiated settlement, but which they do not believe in very strongly—for none of the facts seem to support that hope—and an attitude that totally rejects the prospects opened up by the last war, a reaction of disgust at the incoherent behavior of the various Arab governments, a desire to go back in time to the period before October 1973. The followers of this line feel isolated, abandoned by the other Arabs, thrown back on their own resources. All around them they see the meshes of a plot tightening, woven by all the leaders of the region—Israelis as well as Arabs—getting ready to sacrifice them on the altar of negotiations in which they play no role.

As long as the Israeli leaders maintain the insane attitude of refusing the Palestinians the status of a sovereign people, this second tendency will remain powerful, and from time to time will necessarily lead to acts similar to the ones that took place at Maalot and Kiryat Shemona. In the final analysis, the people who are really responsible for these acts are those who are responsible for the present political stalemate, who deny the Palestinians the simple right to exist. This must be made absolutely clear.

If we deplore these acts, it is because they help to reinforce Israeli intransigence, because they tend to make the Israeli people more open to the arguments of the "diehards," instead of isolating these extremists and allowing for a development of consciousness on the part of the Israeli majority concerning Palestinian national rights. But it is easy to deplore things from a distance, when we are not suffering the same agonies as the Palestinians. Are there other methods of action for them today that would make their voices heard? Only the Palestinians themselves can say. My only certainty is that the currents that are now motivated by this despair would not have popular backing if a clear and honorable solution were offered to the Palestinians, if they felt that their sovereignty were finally recognized by everyone.

SAUL FRIEDLÄNDER: The good faith of the Palestinians concerning their intentions to live peacefully in the future with Israel could be shown right now if they declared that they were ready to put an end to terrorism. The halt of terrorist actions is obviously a precondition for all negotiations. It is not imaginable that the Israeli government would negotiate with Palestinian representatives, while at the same time everyone in Israel was on the lookout for possible assassinations and kidnappings perpetrated by these same Palestinians! But I will go even further. The total halt of terrorist actions is not only an absolute precondition for all negotiations; it must also, in my opinion, correspond to a unilateral decision on the part of the Palestinians to give themselves a different image from the one they have acquired over the past few years.

If the Palestinians want to have even the slightest chance of participating in the process of change that has begun in the Middle East, they must give a moral pledge of their good will and put an immediate end to terrorism.

MAHMOUD HUSSEIN: But it was the Palestinian people who were wronged in the first place. The terrorism was directed against them—at a national level. It is now up to the Israelis to make the first gesture of reconciliation. It is up to those who have tried to deny the existence of this people to give a pledge of good faith—first of all, by recognizing them. You could very easily recognize them as a people with the right to self-determination, even as you condemn the methods used by this or that political current among them. Would you, for example, stipulate as a precondition for recognizing the Egyptian nation that its leaders take action against the Moslem Brotherhood? No. Because the existence of the Egyptian nation is a fact independent of all political contingencies. The Palestinians lack a comparable status. And this explains their present attitude. If, immediately following the October 1973 war, the Israeli leaders had openly recognized the rights of the Palestinian people, there obviously would have been a completely different attitude on the part of Palestinian civilians and resistance fighters.

But your political leaders did not make this gesture, and it seems that they are still very far from wanting to make it. And yet the principal Palestinian leaders have nevertheless taken an important step toward negotiation. At the Palestinian National Council that was held in Cairo in April 1974, they adopted a platform that states that they are ready to go to Geneva on the condition that they are recognized as a separate delegation. They did not say this in so many words, but it is clear to anyone who wants to see. The only response to this was a declaration by Rabin, who stated for the hundredth time: "I have nothing to say to terrorists!"

Terrorism and the Question of Representation

JEAN LACOUTURE: Mahmoud Hussein, you have just said that the platform of the Palestinian National Council was "clear to anyone who wants to see." As long as we give it the benefit of the doubt in a spirit of good will. I'm sure Friedländer does, and certainly you do. Rather than get caught up in complexities of "Palestinology," I would like to ask you, with your knowledge of the situation in Palestine, if you think the main current in the Palestinian movement is now ready to seek a political solution that would lead to a form of coexistence with the State of Israel.

MAHMOUD HUSSEIN: Yes, I think the main current in the resistance movement is ready to seek a solution along those lines and that its principal leaders include this possibility in their vision of the future. But it doesn't depend on them alone. It depends in large part on whether or not Israel is prepared to make this solution plausible by recognizing that they represent a nation. Otherwise, the only possible answer will be Refusal, with a capital R. How could you expect someone like Arafat to present his people with the proposal to negotiate with the Israelis when the Israelis are not satisfied with having scattered the Palestinians to the four corners of the Arab world, but continue to deny their very existence as a nation? That would be the fastest way to demobilize the Palestinians and to lose, in their eyes, all representative character. Until the Israeli leaders present Arafat with a serious basis for discussion, he won't really be able to come forward.

Jean Lacouture, you say that we have to read between the lines of the Palestinian communiqués in a spirit of good will, and I say, "Yes, absolutely, we have to approach them with good will—the Israelis especially, if they want any progress to be made." But if they are simply waiting for the Palestinians' position to change, while their own position has remained the same for twenty-five years, then they can be sure that nothing will happen—or rather, that if anything does happen, it will only result in new confrontations.

SAUL FRIEDLÄNDER: When you say that most Palestinians are in favor of the idea of a peaceful solution, I assume you have in mind the Palestinians who were represented at Cairo and not the ones who refused to go there. Do you think the central organizations, particularly Arafat's, can win out over the extremists? But what is most important now is that you tell us how someone like Arafat would envisage a peaceful solution. Would it be a settlement with Israel as it is now, in other words as a sovereign state, or would it be a solution that involved changes that the Israelis would feel were unacceptable and completely unreasonable?

MAHMOUD HUSSEIN: Let me briefly answer the question about whether those Palestinians prepared to seek a peaceful solution are representatives of all of the Palestinians. They certainly form the majority, but I must point out that they do not have very clearly defined ideas, and that they would only be open to such a solution if it seemed plausible, likely. Since this isn't the case at present, you won't hear explicit statements in favor of it very often. For this group to declare itself openly in favor of a negotiated solution, and for nearly everyone to be behind such a declaration, Israel's position would have to change.

You can't really ask questions like "Will Arafat be able to keep control over all the 'diehards'?" Neither Arafat, nor Sadat, nor

Rabin can do this; not now, and not in the future. Diehards exist everywhere. What matters is the trend of the main current of opinion.

Now let's go on to the second part of your question, which is very important. Once their national rights are restored to them, will the Palestinians envisage coexistence with the State of Israel as it is now? Well, let me say that the Palestinian leaders are far more perceptive than your leaders. They agree to this coexistence, but they know that it can only be unstable and temporary, and that it will have to go much further before it can pave the way for truly peaceful relations between Palestine and Israel.

The ultimate objective of the leaders of the resistance is still to create a single, secular state whose various different communities would flourish together instead of trying to kill each other off. This objective is still very vague, and the steps that will have to be taken to bring it about are still very uncertain, but this is because the concrete conditions in which it will come to pass have hardly begun to form. But the Palestinian leaders persist in it—and I think they are right—because they believe that any other solution, based on two or more states with separate sovereignty, would not be viable.

Let me refer to the opinion of Henry Kissinger, who knows the situation very well. What he said several months ago about the Arab-Israeli conflict—and I quote at second hand—was: "This conflict is a local one which has become regional and then international. I am trying to bring it back down to the regional level and then to the local level. But it is impossible to resolve it completely." In one sense, Kissinger is right. There can be no solution to the conflict as long as the states confronting one another are defiantly nationalist, are based on bourgeois social relations, and are under the rival supervision of the major powers.

This being the case, one could resign oneself to it, as Kissinger does—but that is because once it becomes local it no longer concerns him. Or, like many Israelis, one can choose not to examine the future too closely, or one can dream of an ideal coexistence without worrying about the conditions necessary for it. Or, finally, there is what seems to me the only responsible attitude, that of the Palestinian leaders—to concentrate on the roots of the evil and look for radical remedies instead of being satisfied with palliatives.

Nor should we confine ourselves to formulating optimistic, ideal objectives that are totally abstract as things stand now; what we have to look for are partial, imperfect solutions that can be realized in the near future, solutions that would unblock things, create new possibilities, new ideas about what the last stages might be.

This is what is most productive about the present Palestinian leaders' position. After they posed the long-term goal, they first thought of achieving it by means of an uninterrupted popular war. Then they realized that the formation of a national State of Palestine in just one part of historic Palestine, side by side with the present State of Israel, could constitute a transitional stage; it would not only be more appropriate to the regional and international situation, but also more in keeping with the present aspirations of the Palestinian masses and more amenable to future change.

You cannot take them to task for that, nor can you, before you recognize them, demand a solemn renunciation of objectives which we feel will be forced on us, in the end, by the very situation itself. Israel was established on just one part of a territory which many of you continue to consider the indivisible patrimony, Eretz Yisrael. For people who think in this way the frontiers of 4 June 1967 can only be temporary. That will not prevent the Palestinians from agreeing with the Israelis on conditions for coexistence between the two states, from exchanging reciprocal guarantees and everything that follows from that. It is in keeping with the spirit of the stage envisaged for the near future. But what about afterwards?

Do you seriously think that these two states can live in peace indefinitely while large sections of people within each of them have the feeling they have been cheated out of part of their historic patrimony? While the economy of each of them is founded on the principle of rivalry and that rivalry is completely unequal—Israel being qualitatively ahead of the new Palestinian state? While the politics of each of them depends on the play of influence of the superpowers?

How can you expect a structure like that to hold up? It can only lead to more confrontations unless both sides form a new conception of Arab-Israeli relations. What would be best would be for this conception to lead to more and more deliberate revolutionary disruption contrived by the Arabs and the Israelis themselves, and directed against the ideas, interests, and structures which are perpetuating the mutual hatred.

During a process like this, new bonds would be created between the peoples, formed of mutual tolerance and understanding—and a situation would arise that would encourage the simultaneous flourishing of the different communities.

All I can say is that the formation of a State of Palestine next to the present State of Israel is desirable at this point, but would not represent a miraculous solution. It would be a beginning, but with contradictory possibilities. Take Israel, for example. It was formed in 1948. Were all its problems solved then? Three wars broke out after that. In the same way, the formation of a Palestinian state could just as easily aggravate the contradictions between Arabs and Israelis as it could create a new setting for reciprocal relations, in which the revolutionary political tendencies on both sides would join in the fight against the supervision of the major powers. In any case, I think that in the present context the idea that the creation of the Palestinian state could be a definitive and satisfactory solution is an illusion.

Once the principle is accepted that there will be two rival sovereignties during the years ahead, the only real question which remains to be answered is how the Palestinian revolutionaries envisage the future changes. I think there are two important remarks to be made about this. First of all, they see these changes as taking place with the voluntary, conscious participation of the Israeli masses—and not in opposition to them. The most perceptive among them realize that at this point the fundamental change which they are hoping for is a change in the mood of most Israelis, a capacity on their part to question the repressive structures and the anti-Arab, Western orientation of the State of Israel. And they know that this capacity can only be exercised if the Arabs offer the Israelis the prospect of a common future, to be built together on a new basis.

What will be the new basis? This brings me to my second remark. We must think in terms of a relationship between the Arab and Israeli communities that is flexible and innovative, based on the idea of the sovereignties becoming more and more closely tied while remaining democratic and preventing the oppression of one by the other. You might say that this is a utopian idea. My answer is that only a utopia, in the revolutionary sense of the word, can provide fundamental solutions—and that in any case, the idea of utopia does not scare me. Perhaps here, more than anywhere else, lack of imagination, generosity of spirit, or new perspectives, would be fatal.

What do we mean when we speak of two communities? National communities, or cultural ones, or religious ones? This is where the Palestinians' ideas are not very clear. For many of them, religion is the decisive factor—and that is why they envisage a Jewish community, a Moslem community and even a distinct Christian community. We could even add that the Sephardic Jews and the Ashkenazic Jews form two subcommunities within the Jewish community, in the same way that the Druzes form a separate group within the Moslem community. . .

Like a number of Palestinians, I believe that because of the very special historic circumstances of the region, these groups and subgroups will eventually gather around two main cultural axes, the Judeo-Israeli axis and the Arab-Islamic axis, and any concrete solution that tries to ignore this primary reality will never work. The religion, the culture, the political allegiances, have all defined two basic characters, two realms of collective representation which are certainly far from being unified but which still form two compelling national realities. In seeking formulas for the future, we should take off from here, I think.

But once again, we are talking about the long term and the Palestinian revolutionaries have no definite ideas about it. Over the coming years, the dialogue with the Israelis should certainly help clarify their ideas on this subject.

JEAN LACOUTURE: But what can be said about relations between the Palestinians and Jordan? If a Palestinian state finally comes into being, don't you think it might be more likely to turn toward the East than the West? Wouldn't the idea of stages lead the Palestinians to think of turning toward the other side of the Jordan during the next stage, rather than

toward the Mediterranean? To put it another way, won't the
Palestinians' principal enemy in the coming years be Hussein
rather than Rabin?

MAHMOUD HUSSEIN: The question of relations between Palestine
and Jordan is not a question to be dealt with in the coming years
but rather an immediate question. It is hard to see Hussein, at this
point, as anything but an enemy of the Palestinian resistance. He
has thwarted, and continues to thwart, every step taken by the
resistance toward organizing the Palestinian people, giving it
confidence in itself, representing it in international matters. Right
now he is perhaps even more fiercely opposed than Rabin to the
PLO being recognized as the spokesman for the whole of
Palestine—simply because most of his kingdom is peopled by
Palestinians and if the PLO were recognized, he himself would be
representing so few people as to become ludicrous.

    Yet the PLO hardly lays down the law in the Arab world. Since
for the moment Hussein is protected by Washington and backed by
Arab leaders like Faisal and Sadat, Arafat may be compelled, in
spite of everything, to draw up more or less temporary compromise
solutions with Hussein. How far might such compromises go? Will
the Hashemite kingdom itself last much longer?

    When the Palestinian state comes into being, will it be an
entirely autonomous entity? Or will it form part of a Palestinian-
Jordanian federation, or even a Syrian-Palestinian-Jordanian federation? These are the unanswered questions. No one can answer them
beforehand, because the situation is still very changeable, the
balance of inter-Arab forces is certainly going to change over the
course of the next few years, and any possible agreements are
going to be affected by these changes. What is certain is that the
antagonism of the Palestinian revolutionaries toward the Hashemite
throne is just as deep as their antagonism toward the Zionist
government, and that they will have their hands full defending the
Palestinian sovereignty on both fronts during the next phase.

SAUL FRIEDLÄNDER: What you say about how the Palestinians see
future relations with Israel is really very ambiguous. Listening to
you, one doesn't know whether the emphasis should be on their

agreeing to let the two sovereign states coexist for the moment, leaving the profound changes you foresee to an indeterminate and vague future, or whether the present coexistence is only seen as a brief tactical stage that would allow the Palestinians to resume the attack on the State of Israel within a short time. It is a little like the Soviet Union on a smaller scale. We don't know if coexistence with the capitalist world is a definitive reality, and world-wide revolution simply a slogan, or if coexistence is only seen as one phase—intended to deceive the capitalists and prepare more effectively for world-wide revolution. Actually, I think the Communists themselves are not very clear about the answer to that, nor are the Palestinians. So I won't press you about prospects for the future, but you should know that everything you said can be interpreted in two ways, and that if ever a serious negotiation is begun with the Palestinians, the Israelis will not be satisfied with such vague statements.

The discussion about the present and the future has prevented me from commenting on what you said about the roots of the conflict with the Palestinians, about the question of fundamental rights, about the problems of justice and injustice. I would like to make my thoughts clear on this point, and then I will tell you how the political solution to the Palestinian question is specifically envisaged in Israel, and how I envisage it myself.

To begin with, without beating around the bush, I will say that objectively the Palestinians have suffered an injustice, even if it wasn't voluntarily inflicted. I don't need to repeat that I recognize the existence of a Palestinian people, at least one that is in the process of taking shape. But just because the Palestinians have suffered, it does not mean that Zionism must be questioned. As far as I can see, it would be just as unjust to refuse the Jews the right to realize their age-old bond with the land of Israel. As I said in my book on the future of Israel, the tragedy lies in the fact that two causes are confronting one another that are both inherently right, each in its own way, each on its own level.

The Palestinians' bond with the land of Palestine is obvious, but confronting this right is a completely different sort of right, perhaps a right *sui generis*, the Jews' right to realize their ties to the land of Israel, because the Jewish people define themselves as a people only by their ties to this land. Here I am only repeating what I explained to you at the beginning of our dialogue.

During their entire existence in Diaspora for almost two thousand years, the Jews have felt driven out, dispersed, exiled from this ancestral land, which they longed to return to. This is unique in history. I think that such a strong bond, such a fundamental bond, gives this people a right to this land. Only the Jews have placed such a high value on it and considered it irreplaceable, even if for a time—and that time lasted centuries—they lived in other places.

The Law of Return

JEAN LACOUTURE: Speaking as a historian, not just as an Israeli citizen, Saul Friedländer, could you answer one question. Is the notion of a Jewish people in Diaspora entirely defensible, is it scientifically admissible? Do you believe the Jews of Ethiopia, Vitebsk, Istanbul and Vilna all belonged, or still belong, to one people? Is a shared religious and historic tradition, however fondly nurtured, however painfully suffered, enough to constitute a "people" if the tradition is expressed in many different languages?

SAUL FRIEDLÄNDER: You are asking a fundamental question and I think it has only one possible answer. As far as I'm concerned the answer is yes, once the term people is defined in a particular way. In this case the definition is not based on geographic criteria, but on the feeling of sharing a common past, a common history, of being both linked by and devoted to a common destiny. I would say that with slight differences the situation of Jews in Diaspora was more or less the same in their different countries. At any one time the persecutions in one country might have been more intense than in another, but by and large the fate of the Jews in a Christian world or in a Moslem world has been unique, experienced in isolation, and shared by other Jews. Finally, Jews have had certain aspirations in common, first a religious vision of the future, and then, starting in the nineteenth century, a national religious vision.

Moreover, the Jewish religion is a national religion, which from its very beginning has been practiced by a small group of people with a long national history. The Jews do not make an absolute distinction between religion and nationality. Of course, certain Jewish ideas are of a universal nature, but there is also a bond among the people who have been "chosen" by God—though they are still a people—to carry a certain message. The people, therefore, is responsible for the message, and the religious element is tied to the existence of the people, and this people feels indissolubly tied to a certain land. The religion, the people, and the land form an indivisible unit in authentic Jewish thought.

Over the centuries many Jews have tried to dissociate themselves from this national-religious "ideology," and therefore from Judaism as such, but those who have remained part of the Jewish people have more or less explicitly accepted this belonging in both religious and national terms, even though these terms are quite special.

JEAN LACOUTURE: You haven't yet talked about language, which is an essential element in a community. Modern Hebrew, the masterpiece of modern Judaism, must have been elaborated in the process of creating, or in order to create, the State of Israel.

SAUL FRIEDLÄNDER: That's quite right. You are using certain criteria to define a people—the land and the language. I have other criteria, particularly one which I consider fundamental—a people exists when any group of individuals feels it is a people and wants to be a people. It is possible to live in the same land and speak the same language, and yet belong to different peoples. Take the Belgians and the French. They both speak French and they live side by side on the same territory—the frontier between them is purely political. Well! The Belgians feel Belgian and the French feel French. Similarly, it is possible to be widely scattered, to live in New York, Sydney, or Jerusalem, and yet feel part of one people. National feeling is something that is essentially subjective. Some people feel they are members of the Polish people, even though they live in Milwaukee, for example. There is a real difference between the fact of citizenship and the feeling of belonging to a people. A person can be a French citizen and yet feel he belongs to the Jewish people.

MAHMOUD HUSSEIN: The view of history you have just given us is really too simplistic, and what is worse, it attributes a sort of *a priori* inevitability to the process that led to Zionism, and there is no basis in fact for this. It may be true that the Jewish religion is a national religion and that return to Jerusalem is the rallying cry of the dispersed Jews, but it wasn't inevitable that this should lead to the creation of a Jewish state in Palestine. You must be well aware that for a long time, within Jewish communities, the people who wanted to give a temporal meaning to the cry "next year in Jerusalem" were thwarted by the ones who wanted to preserve its uniquely spiritual meaning.

For centuries Jews have lived in their different adoptive countries without considering returning to the land of their religious ancestors. After the liberal bourgeois revolution, which broke down the strict religious barriers, the tendency of the Jews to assimilate was an undeniable fact. It was in the countries where they were persecuted in one way or another that political Zionism came into being, and you know very well that even after the Balfour Declaration only a minority of the Jews in the world followed the lead of the Zionist movement.

Not until Nazism did a majority of the Jews in the West become attached to the idea of a Jewish state in Palestine, and most of them did not feel the need to emigrate. Then the trouble caused in the Arab countries by the creation of Israel made the Jews of the East begin to feel that they also were concerned, and some of them went to swell the population of Israel. So that a series of particular historical events, none of which was inevitable, was needed before Israel could be adopted by the majority of Jews in the world. Zionism is one interpretation among others of the Jewish hope, a historically dated, politically identified interpretation. In any case, it does not provide any justification for the fifteen million Jews of the world assembling in Palestine.

SAUL FRIEDLÄNDER: Let's not jump from one subject to another. At
this point we're not concerned with whether or not fifteen million
Jews should go to Israel. The deeper problem is a different one.
I'm well aware that there have been attempts to assimilate. Jews
have tried to find a place in the liberal bourgeois world; they have
tried to find the solution to their problems in socialism, a form of
socialism which would have completely cut them off from Judaism.
All this is well known. I am not presenting a simplified account of
Jewish history here, I am trying once again to describe briefly what
the roots of Zionism were, *the way of thinking that became
Zionism*.

This way of thinking always existed—on a purely religious level
first, then on a secular level—and this sense of continuity between
the concept of the Jewish religion and the concept of the Jewish
nation was most evident among the poor Jews of Central and
Eastern Europe. When the founder of political Zionism, Theodor
Herzl, had the idea—an unfortunate one, given the Jewish
context—of suggesting a territorial solution other than
Palestine—Uganda, as you know—he provoked a general outcry,
particularly on the part of the delegates from the masses of Jewish
people in Eastern Europe. They were unanimous in saying, "There
is only one place to go, and that is Palestine, *Eretz Yisrael*!" You
can see that there is a very close link between the traditional
religious attitude and the modern nationalist one; they have many
of the same characteristics. Moreover, this is not an exclusively
Jewish pattern; it can be seen in the transition from a certain kind
of Slavic orthodoxy to a certain kind of modern Slavic nationalism,
not to mention the relation between Arab nationalism and Islam.

I explicitly recognize a Palestinian reality which has become a
national reality with certain rights to assert on a particular land. But
I must point out that confronting that reality, on another level
because its evolution has been different, is a Jewish national
reality, however complex its foundations, which has had an almost
continuous bond—expressed sometimes in one way and sometimes
in another—with a particular land. It is motivated by a will to
return which was not fulfilled for a long time, since in the existing
circumstances it was not clear what form the fulfillment should
take. I will repeat what I said a few years ago. Two rights of

different kinds are confronting one another. That is the whole problem.

MAHMOUD HUSSEIN: My remark about the fifteen million Jews of the world assembling in Israel was not made lightly. Since you speak of a Jewish people, whatever the criteria you use for defining a people—and I don't want to enter into a discussion of that here—that definition must necessarily include a certain implicit desire, one which can possibly remain unanswered for a long time but which may also just as well, in certain exceptional circumstances, be fulfilled in the end—the aspiration to gather this people within one single land under the authority of one single state. You must realize what a problem that creates.

SAUL FRIEDLÄNDER: We are therefore confronted with two rights that are equal and antagonistic. Now we have to try to see how this problem can be solved. It is perhaps the most difficult element—certainly the most fundamental element—in the Arab-Israeli conflict. I believe this conflict is taking place in three areas: there is an outside circle, involving the foreign powers in the region; then the first inner circle, involving the different states of the region; then the innermost circle, where the people of Israel confront the Palestinian people. I don't think the conflict can be resolved without touching the innermost circle.

MAHMOUD HUSSEIN: What do you mean by "the people of Israel"? Are they the same as what you called the "Jewish people" or are they the present inhabitants of the State of Israel?

SAUL FRIEDLÄNDER: When I say "the people of Israel," in this case I am referring to the people living in Israel.

I could extricate myself from this problem very easily by saying to you that after all this is not a new situation. History has witnessed other populations being displaced, other "colonizations" which were irreversible—because actually the colonizations that took place during the nineteenth century aren't the only familiar ones. I am not just talking about the French in Algeria or the English in various part of Africa (these were temporary situations which eventually were brought back to their starting point). There were earlier periods: the Europeans in America—and just because the Indian population was sparse and the culture not very structured, one can't pretend the Indians didn't exist. Similarly, we could say, "What about the United States, New Zealand, Australia, not to mention Latin America?" If I wanted to, I could very easily rely on facile arguments and say, "After all, this is nothing new! There has been an injustice, and it's tragic, but history has witnessed many injustices, history is full of migrations, the migration of the Jews is just one more. The others are irreversible and it's more or less the same with Israel! Too bad for the Palestinians. Over the years this will provoke violent hostility, but if Israel can defend itself against that hostility, I don't see any reason to worry about it..."

This is an argument I won't use, for two reasons.

I have already touched on the first. I think the conflict between Israel and the Arab peoples will not come to an end until a solution to the Palestinian problem has been found which everyone can accept. An unending conflict would lead to the annihilation of both sides. So I think at all costs the Palestinian problem must be solved.

There is another reason, which I'm sure you haven't thought of and which is related to my view of Zionism. As I see it, Zionism is more than just a national movement. Zionism emanates from a religious conception, a spiritual conception developed by the Jewish people. But certain notions, certain values, are implicit in the idea of religion. Now as you know, the Jewish religion is particularist, but it also has universalist aspects which imply fundamental moral values, especially the idea of justice.

Because of this, Zionism has always been more than simply a national return for me; it has tried to establish a certain kind of society and promote certain moral values. The idea of justice has been a central element within it. We could put it this way—justice for the Jews first of all, yes, but justice for other people too. Personally, I could not imagine Zionism being founded on an injustice. Over the years this would eat away at it from inside. So not only for moral reasons, but also for the very survival of Zionism, it seems to me essential to find a just solution to the Palestinian problem.

The arguments I am using have a bearing on the conflict, but they also take into account our own aspirations, which go beyond purely national concerns.

As for concrete solutions to the problem, there is a whole range of suggestions in Israel. For example, it would be wrong to think that the nationalist right wing, particularly the Likud, has nothing to propose concerning the Palestinians. They believe Palestine was artificially divided by the English in 1922; up to then it included both Palestine and Transjordan. They feel that the Palestinians ought to establish their state on the part of the territory that represented more than half of Palestine before 1922, in other words, Transjordan.

There is another solution, probably advocated by the greatest number of people today, and that is the one expressed by the present government. The reasoning behind it is more or less this. Since the great majority of Palestinians live either in Jordan proper (which is geographically Transjordan), or on the occupied West Bank, a solution could be conceived of in a Jordanian-Palestinian political context. Israel would negotiate with Jordan and give most of the West Bank directly back to it. Jordan itself has proposed the establishment of a Jordano-Palestinian federation. It is likely that in the long run this federation would be transformed, for demographic and political reasons, into a Palestinian state. In this way Jordan would be progressively Palestinized.

This conception seems to have some positive aspects. I myself reject it, not in principle but for practical reasons: *any negotiation with the Jordanians alone would not involve the Palestinians*. Now the Palestinization of Jordan or the secession of the West Bank, followed by the formation of an independent Palestinian state, could take place more quickly than one would think. If this were to happen, Israel would find itself confronting a Palestinian state with which it had not had preliminary negotiations and which would therefore not be bound by any obligations in its dealings with the Jewish state. Obviously that situation must be avoided.

There is a third possibility, which I myself am in favor of: the division of ex-mandatory Palestine into two states, an Israeli state and a Palestinian state. More specifically, there would be a State of Israel within the frontiers of 4 June 1967, except for a few adjustments (the return to these frontiers would be carried out in stages, as I described it). The West Bank, which is occupied by Israel now, and in time the Gaza Strip too, would make up the Palestinian state, which could extend to Transjordan later. But all this would be subject to one express condition, one *sine qua non*. The leaders of the Palestinian state which might be created on the West Bank would have to declare explicitly and in an unequivocal manner that they were prepared to live in peace with the State of Israel and that for them the creation of a Palestinian state on the West Bank and in the Gaza Strip was not the first stage in a process whose second stage would be the destruction of the State of Israel or the replacement of the Jewish state by a "secular and democratic" Palestine, which is the same thing in the end. They would have to declare in an absolutely unequivocal manner that in their eyes the newly created State of Palestine was the end of the road.

MAHMOUD HUSSEIN: Many things strike me about your account. For example, you said the Palestinians must recognize the State of Israel as it is, and that they must not see this recognition as a transitional stage but as the end of the road.

Tell us, as a historian, if there has ever been an end of the road. Even in a state like Egypt, which is recognized by everyone, we cannot speak of the end of the road, we cannot block off the future and dismiss the possibility, for example, of Egypt uniting with other states. What strikes me most is your fixation on the sanctity of the structures of the present State of Israel, whereas at other times you stress the necessity of Israel becoming integrated into the region. How could it really become integrated without changing?

SAUL FRIEDLÄNDER: The meaning of what I said is very clear. It would be incumbent upon the Palestinian leaders who take on the responsibility of representing their people to say that they will not tolerate violent and hostile activities against Israel within their country, that they will not allow their state to serve as a stepping stone for saboteurs, who would otherwise infiltrate Israel with the backing of their authority in a sense. These leaders will have to make it very clear that their intention is simply to live in peace with Israel. Obviously the Palestinians can't guarantee anything about the distant future, but neither can Israel...

MAHMOUD HUSSEIN: I could understand it if you asked that the Palestinians not try to change the established relations between their state and yours by force. But what harm do you see in these relations being modified, if they are modified with the consent of the Palestinians and the Israelis or a large number of them? Which leads us to a reversal of the terms of the problem as it was posed, because the ones who have all the qualifications of a sovereign state at the moment are the Israelis, whereas the Palestinians do not have anything remotely like a sovereign state.

For a long time, the only ones able to change an agreement by force will be the Israelis. Then the question I ask you, Friedländer, is this. How do you envisage the sovereign State of Palestine whose creation you are proposing? We are aware of the weight of mutual mistrust that has accumulated between the Palestinians and the Israelis and which can only be dispelled gradually, starting with an exchange of serious guarantees by both sides. You insist on the need for these guarantees, but one has the impression that the guarantees you are really thinking of are the ones the Israelis expect from the Palestinians. You actually seem to be very insistent about this; you don't place much faith in the promises of the great powers, or in the international treaties!

The fact is that the only truly reassuring guarantees, as long as the historic distrust still remains, are those inherent in the balance of forces in the region. The guarantee represented by the ability to defend oneself against the pressure of the adversary. You, yourself, have said this many times. Then I ask you, do you think that a sovereign Palestinian state has the same right to defend itself that you think Israel should have?

SAUL FRIEDLÄNDER: In principle, yes, but in practice there would have to be a series of partial and temporary arrangements to normalize relations between the two states. Besides, in this case heavy arms would not be involved. The Palestinian state would not be able to marshal armored divisions against Israel. The real problem from Israel's point of view is infiltration and sabotage. I don't know what kinds of concrete measures we would have to resort to in order to prevent any infiltration, but it is obviously a very important issue.

MAHMOUD HUSSEIN: As you know, there are intermediate solutions to the problem you pose. Parallel zones can be created where both sides are less heavily armed and are only more heavily armed as they get farther away from the line separating the forces. What is important to find out is if you think arms limitation, whether progressive or not, should be imposed on Israel as well as on the Palestinian state, or only on the Palestinian state. You ought to be aware of the fact that Palestinian mistrust of Israel is at least as profound as your mistrust of the Palestinians. Anyway, you can't prevent the Palestinian state from joining forces with Jordan at some point in the future, or even with the State of Syria, in a federation, thus giving itself much greater strategic depth than you have. Under these circumstances, will you demand that you always be better armed than the Palestinian state? It could be said that in each of these cases, the ideal for you would be an unarmed Palestinian state, a sort of buffer zone between you and the other Arab states. Needless to say, this would be unacceptable to the Palestinians.

SAUL FRIEDLÄNDER: This is not what I meant, but it is true that the limited extent of the regions we are talking about poses a problem. But I don't think it is necessary to go into this kind of detail. These are really questions for specialists in military affairs to deal with; it is up to them to see how a demilitarized zone might be established in the present situation, or a buffer zone, or even a corridor placed under the supervision of UN forces.

MAHMOUD HUSSEIN: But let us at least lay down one essential principle for the future. Everything that concerns the Palestinians will have to be discussed with the Palestinians. All I can do here is emphasize the issues which seem to me most important from the Palestinians' point of view. So let us approach the future from another direction. When I say that the principal leaders of the PLO are ready to accept the idea of a State of Palestine existing side by side with the present State of Israel, it should be understood that in their eyes this would not affect a fundamental aspiration of the Palestinians, wherever they might find themselves when the time came—the aspiration to be able to move freely over the whole of historic Palestine, in order to visit, of course, but also in order to work there eventually, and even live there. I think this feeling is irrepressible and is going to determine many things in the future. even if a Palestinian state is created in part of Palestine.

You ought to understand this feeling, since you are convinced that for nearly two thousand years the Jews in Diaspora have felt an ineradicable aspiration to return to Zion. The Palestinians have been separated for more than two decades from the land which has become Israel. Their hopes for returning are certainly no less deeply rooted in their collective consciousness, and these hopes will end by paving the way, somehow, to their realization. Then, if you understand this feeling, you should see that solutions that would satisfy it must be sought together, once Palestinian sovereignty has been recognized.

From this point of view, I think it would be very important for Israel to declare, even in the abstract, that in principle the Palestinians have a right to return—and for Israel to be ready to discuss with great care how this right might be fulfilled.

That would upset the whole psychology of relations between the Israelis and the Palestinians. Do you think that this sort of declaration of principle is foreseeable.?

SAUL FRIEDLÄNDER: My answer necessarily reverts back to Zionism, or at least to one of its essential aspects. The Zionist idea implies that there will be a place on earth—which happens to be Israel—where Jews will be sovereign, masters of their fate, and will therefore necessarily form a majority. Obviously, anything which tended to challenge this sovereignty within the agreed upon limits of Israel would be inadmissible; the very essence of the Zionist project would be threatened. The democratic exercise of sovereignty requires, in this case, that there be an incontestable majority of Jews—I wouldn't say homogeneity of population, since as you know there are five hundred thousand Arabs living within the frontiers of the State of Israel at the moment. What is more, the Arab population within Israel is growing more rapidly than the Jewish population; at the present rate, it is possible that by the time there are four million Jews, the number of Israeli Arabs will have risen to seven or eight hundred thousand, perhaps even a million.

So that even within the State of Israel, the Arab population is already a substantial minority. Because of this, it would not be reasonable to consider the possibility of a great many more Arabs moving into Israel; that would threaten the very character of the Jewish state.

MAHMOUD HUSSEIN: Yet that is one way of applying Dayan's proposal, which you described the day before yesterday, to the Palestinian situation. I said to you then in principle it wasn't bad, but that what worried me was that it came from Dayan. The essential thing to realize is that if you recognize the Jews' right to settle in a territory which they consider to be a historic patrimony, then how can you fail to recognize the same right for the Palestinians? So that once the principle of two similar sovereignties has been established, what we have to do is fulfill the particular aspirations, because if they are not fulfilled willingly, cooperatively, they will end by imposing themselves in quite a different way. We will have to try, therefore, to compose basic formulas in which territorial boundaries will be only one element among many in the very complex formulas that will have to be worked out to resolve the problem of relations between the Palestinians and the Israelis.

SAUL FRIEDLÄNDER: I agree with the way you formulate things. I will go even further and actually take up Dayan's idea again. What he says is that whatever the political agreement, the Jews should be able to go and settle in Jericho, Hebron, and the other places which have important emotional significance for them. Then why won't the Arabs coming from the West Bank, in this case, settle near Jaffa if they really want to? Once there are two sovereign states, they will have their own laws governing immigration and they will have the power to control the settling of foreigners, but the right to visit will remain incontestable.

It is inconceivable that Palestine be divided into two sovereign states without anyone being allowed to cross the borders. That would be intolerable. Obviously, because of the small size of the territory, everyone must be able to visit the whole of the country whenever he likes. But the right to settle is a more complicated business. Besides, I don't think there will be many Jews wanting to settle in Jericho or Hebron, and there won't be thousands of Palestinians wanting to settle in densely populated Jewish territory, because they would feel completely out of their natural social context.

MAHMOUD HUSSEIN: For all Arabs, the law of return is the symbol of the plundering of Palestine. Until now it has implied both the Jewish immigration and the Palestinian exodus. What makes Dayan's proposition unacceptable in the present context is the fact that the Palestinians are still very far from having a recognized sovereign state. But if that state comes into being and then arrives at an understanding with Israel on how to resolve the problem posed on both sides by immigration, and on the balances that will have to be respected, and above all on the ways to prevent Jewish immigration from turning into expansion of Israel, then who will be able to object?

SAUL FRIEDLÄNDER: Obviously the law of return has a very different meaning for us. I think something that is really very simple is being made complicated here. Suppose we have two sovereign states in Palestine, in accordance with the idea which both you and I have formed. The Palestinians are sovereign in their state, the Israelis in theirs. It is clear that people will be able to travel from one place to the other, and some will eventually be able to settle in the neighboring state. We have agreed on all this. As for the law of return, it allows every Jew who so wishes to settle in Israel, since that is Israel's very reason for existing. But how could that bother the Palestinians, since it involves Israel, within its own frontiers? This is the Israel we are talking about. It is something agreed upon, evident, clear. In my opinion the number of Jews could be multiplied several times and it wouldn't change anything. As my friend Eliav says—and I share some of his ideas—we will build Israel in height and in depth. Why not? That shouldn't bother anyone, not even Palestinian Arabs who would like to come and settle in Israel. Nowadays, we have gone beyond that kind of demographic problem (I won't try to say anything about the problem on a planetary scale).

And what exactly are we talking about? In a purely hypothetical situation, it could happen that all of a sudden all the Jews in the world were threatened or persecuted. In such an imaginary situation, they would have every right to come and settle in Israel. The State of Israel would have to manage to integrate them within the limits of its frontiers. But we are not talking about imaginary situations, we are talking about the real situation. The real situation, as far as we can see, is that forty or fifty thousand immigrants arrive in Israel every year. There could be as many as seventy thousand. . .there have been as few as fifteen thousand. Before the 1967 war the rate of immigration went down considerably. There was actually more emigration than immigration. Now, because of the particular situation of the Jews of the Soviet Union, it is expected that tens of thousands of Russian Jews will come each year. There are still some Jews coming from the Middle East or the North African countries; a handful of others arrive from Western Europe or Latin America; a very small number from the United States. As I said, it is a matter of fifty of sixty thousand people a year; it could go up somewhat; it could also easily go down. Even when the immigration figures are added to the natural growth of the Israeli population, the total may still be lower than the natural growth of the Palestinian population. There is nothing here to worry anyone, and even if many more immigrants were forced to come, because of situations that can't be predicted at this point, it would be the duty of the State of Israel to receive them and its problem to find room for them to live within its legal and recognized frontiers.

MAHMOUD HUSSEIN: It is difficult to be convinced by your assurances. You are fond of repeating that things should not be simplified, and you're right. But that applies to everything, including the Palestinians' feeling of frustration. Imagine millions of Russian or American Jews landing in Israel under the pressure of some extraordinary international event. Do you think you could reassure the Palestinians at that point by repeating to them that this concerned only you, that they shouldn't be afraid you would enlarge your territory again? And they, in their little Palestinian state which you think should remain without effective means of defending itself, are supposed to take your word for it, and rely on the good faith of the Israeli administration? As if precisely that same administration had not driven them from their home in the first place? The Palestinians' confidence in the Israelis will need much more than promises like that before it can become deeply rooted. Here you are putting the cart before the horse when you imagine that the problem of confidence has already been solved—when actually it will be the central problem between you for a very long time if you begin trying to coexist.

As for the premise of your reasoning, it is extremely naive. You say that Israel could integrate fifteen million Jews by building up and digging down. If it were only a question of the technical aspect of a plan like that, I wouldn't be very worried about it. But an economic structure which allows you to build Israel on the model of New York or Tokyo would be a capitalist structure. The fifteen million Jews could only be integrated as a productive force, which would have to be used in a rational, profitable manner. A high level of technology and a high profit—on a capitalist basis—would necessarily pose the problem of markets, of the vital flow of production which could not be absorbed on the spot. Besides, this is a problem already. Imagine what it would be if you multiplied Israel's productive capacity several times!

You will say that markets can be found everywhere—in Africa, Latin America, elsewhere. Yes, but these markets are not untouched, they are already sought after by many competitors who are in a better position than Israel for various reasons. The only natural market, so to speak, in which Israeli products would have an advantage over other competitors, would be the economically backward Arab world. The Israeli leaders are well aware of this, realizing the organic importance of exchanges between Israel and the West Bank. In all their statements concerning the Arab-Israeli negotiations, they emphasize the need to open the economic frontiers on both sides.

But given the present levels of development, and if the economic structure of the region remains capitalist, this would result in an unequal relationship. Israel would become the industrial and technological center of the Middle East at the expense of the Arab bourgeoisies.

I have already shown how Egypt under Nasser made a stand against this sort of prospect. There can be no ambiguity where this is concerned—Egyptian capitalism is a potential rival of Israeli capitalism. Of course, Egypt is at a disadvantage at the technological and organizational level, but on the other hand, it has the advantage of being part of the Arab cultural universe and is considered the guardian of independence and unification of the region against foreign interference.

This rivalry would become even more merciless, if a certain possibility were realized—it is still vague at the moment but I think it has a good chance of being realized if there is a period of political coexistence between the Arabs and the Israelis. This is the possibility of an inter-Arab economic rapprochement, a form of regional Arab power. It cannot come to pass without some political upheavals, but it would answer a desire that is growing in the Arab bourgeoisies. The Faisal-Sadat axis may be the prefiguration of it.

There is a good chance that the Israeli bourgeoisie would then try to oppose this tendency, and make the usual statements: Arab power threatens Israel's security, the Arabs refuse to accept Israel, etc. But how could it be any other way? There are many Arab businessmen, and some Arab governments have immense financial means. Why would they give the Israeli capitalists a chance to outstrip them or supplant them in their own territory?

For the Arab masses, this competition would seem like one more episode in the fight between national independence and foreign supervision. If Israeli capitalism exerted a greater and greater influence over the Arab world, if the center of economic decision were to become Tel Aviv rather than Cairo, Damascus, or Riyadh—a pattern would be repeating itself that was very familiar and had become intolerable. Israel would be filling the shoes of the old colonialists. It would be laying down the law to the Arabs in their own countries; it would, in fact, have exchanged the military occupation of certain Arab territories for economic occupation of the entire region. Everything would have to begin all over again.

The Sabras and the Future

JEAN LACOUTURE: As we approach the final phase of these discussions and begin to draw our conclusions, I would like to make two observations, which will develop into two questions, addressed to the two participants.

First observation: What makes for such difficulties in finding a political solution in the Middle East, among other things, is the fact that we are dealing with two different dynamic principles. The adjustment between the two entities or groups in question is not a matter of bringing together two stationary and inert objects which can be neatly fitted into place, but two forces in motion.

Mahmoud Hussein has just reminded us of the fact that the Arab-Palestinian force is above all moved by a feeling of frustration, by a desire to accelerate the action, which has been so slow in the past, and to be given what it feels it deserves; the Palestinian leaders, even the peaceful ones, do not speak of an end, but of stages. The Palestinian national principle resides in polemic, struggle, and emotion. There is nothing more difficult to grasp, to understand, to define. Nothing that so little lends itself to negotiation, written agreement, and restructuring. On the other side, Israel too, in its very essence, is a force in motion, an evolution of forms.

By definition Zionism is dynamic, and this is one of its aspects that makes it difficult for Arabs to understand and accept.

In general, the history of the last few years can be summed up as follows. The Arabs, after having violently rejected the very idea of Israel and having more or less allied themselves with "Shukairyism" under the slogan of "driving the Jews into the sea," then accepted the *Yishuv*, the establishment of a large Jewish population in the Middle East, the formula of a large "democratic, secular, and multireligious state," which meant that they accepted the permanent presence of the Jewish people in the Middle East. In some sense, this was a step forward...Then the great majority of the Arab political leaders acknowledged the principle of coexistence with the State of Israel within its June 1967 borders.

The problem now is whether or not the Arab world is ready to accept the State of Israel as a manifestation and expression of Zionism. Friedländer gave us some valuable insights into the way we can conceive of Zionism today—whose purpose isn't literally to bring together as quickly as possible the whole Jewish population of the world in this small territory. But however one understands Zionism, it obviously poses an essential problem to the Arab world, just as militant Arab-Palestinianism poses a problem to Israel.

To what extent can these two dynamic forces be considered compatible with the coexistence that is being sought?

SAUL FRIEDLÄNDER: You are asking me how Israel can be integrated into the Middle East. You are asking what the elements are that in the long run can lead us to believe in an increasing harmony in the relations between the State of Israel, with its Zionist foundation, and the neighboring Arab world, with its particular characteristics—which we have discussed at great length during the past three days.

I am tempted to end this debate with the description of what could be the harmonious relations of the future. But I think that our realism during this discussion forces me to moderate my hopes concerning the process of normalizing and harmonizing our relations. This, in fact, is the reason why I can't think of any political settlement that would not be gradual.

But if the normalization of political relations can be accomplished within a few years, the normalization of human relations, the harmonizing of two such different types of society, will probably take considerably more time, and concerning this nothing is certain. In my book on the future of Israel I described the gap between the two societies, as well as all the profound divergences. The elements of convergence that I am going to mention now do not have the same weight. Nevertheless, they are there—without overemphasizing their importance, I should point them out. If it's all right with you, I will first talk about the least tangible factors and then about the more concrete ones.

Perhaps you remember that shortly before the 1967 war a book by Georges Friedmann entitled *End of the Jewish People?* was published in Paris. Friedmann's thesis made a big stir at the time. He contended that something special was taking place in Israel, something specifically Israeli that was diverging more and more from the Judaism of the Diaspora, and in such a way that soon there would be little or nothing in common between the Israelis and the Israeli experience and the rest of the Jewish world. For this reason he asked the question: Is this the end of the Jews as a single and united people? In 1966, when the book appeared, many people wondered whether or not Friedmann hadn't put his finger on a fundamental development. . .The war that followed showed that he had been wrong, and that when the moment of danger came there was an enormous outburst of shared emotion in favor of unity, and that the underlying bond felt by all Jews conscious of being Jews was finally more important than the nature of this or that characteristic of the Israelis as compared to the Jews of the Diaspora. I think that the idea of an underlying bond is fundamentally correct, but even so, I think that in Israel there is something happening, something in the process of being formed, a kind of sensibility developing that will give Israeli society—without cutting it off from the Diaspora—specific characteristics that will facilitate the rapprochement we are talking about.

First of all, in a general manner, we are witnessing the birth of what I would call a "new man." Without resorting to big words or high-flown phrases, there is no question that this is an authentic phenomenon (you know that there is a particular term, Sabra, used to indicate an Israeli born in Israel). From the fact that he has been born in the Middle East, and not in Poland, or Russia, or America, the Sabra feels at home in the same physical surroundings as the Arab. In some sense he breathes the same air and also understands, in most cases, the same language (the Sabra, of course, speaks Hebrew, but he also often understands Arabic, which is taught in school). Contacts with the Arab population are more or less natural.

In the eyes of the Sabra, the Arab is less invested with the myth and mystery he has had and still has for the immigrant. And then, there is a characteristic of the Sabras that made a strong impression on me during the Six Day War (I spoke of this in the last chapter of my book on the future of Israel), a particular type of sensibility, the Jewish sensibility in its finest form—an ability to identify with the misfortunes of others. Perhaps you remember the interviews with soldiers, young people from the kibbutzim, young people in their twenties from all over the country, who expressed the real situation of the Arabs and the misfortune of the Palestinians better than anyone up to now. Aside from the Arab literature on this subject— it is no doubt much more intense, but I am not familiar with it—these are the most moving statements I have read on the reality of Palestinian suffering.

Allow me to repeat several lines at random from the "interviews with soldiers,"* from the dozens of texts I quoted. This is Menachem of *Ein-Hahoresh* speaking: "It was painful for me to be in an army of occupation, in a strong and victorious army. I suddenly understood what the Second World War and the Holocaust must have been like when I was going up the road from Jericho to Jerusalem and the refugees were going down in the opposite direction... I identified with them totally. When I saw those children in their parents' arms... I almost saw myself being carried by my own father... This was probably the most tragic thing of all, this identification with another people, with our enemies..."

*Translated into English and published in book form as *The Seventh Day*, edited by Avraham Shapira.

Finally, in the new generation, among the Sabras who are reaching maturity in 1974, there is a tendency to call everything into question. There are no more taboos in Israel; people approach subjects in a highly critical manner. The young Israeli today asks questions that ten or fifteen years ago would have been considered absolutely sacrilegious. This is the good side of Israeli society—it lets people express themselves, and among the young people we can see a desire for radical questioning, a fundamental examination of things. I see in all this, of course, an infinitely greater possibility for understanding others than in the ideologues who are still shut in by the old ideas of twenty, thirty, or fifty years ago, and who until very recently dominated the Israeli scene. Little by little these young Sabras are coming into positions of power.

I have another point to make. It is true that the Zionist State of Israel can arouse certain fears among the Arabs, because of its dynamism and its tendency, not toward expansion—I must emphasize that —but toward continuous strengthening because of the arrival of people from very different backgrounds. The permanence of the Zionist objective, which undoubtedly raises a psychological barrier to Israel's integration into the area, can be considered in a completely different light.

Among the immigrants, there are many whose choice has been motivated by idealism—in many cases by religious idealism, it is true, and often it is undeniably conservative. But some of them, who like to stir up ideas of social change (and this is an inherent characteristic of Zionism) come with new options in mind. In this way, indirectly, because of Israel, elements which you would readily consider revolutionary are entering the Middle East, and from your point of view—though not necessarily from mine—they may not only challenge the present state of things, but think of solutions whose tenor and scope would lead us way beyond our current conceptions.

If I had to sum up Israel's role as I see it today and as I hope to see it develop in the future, I would say that because of the rise of a new generation and the flowering of a new sensibility, and also because of Israel's role as a "communicating vessel" between the Jewish people and all that it inspires in the realm of ideas, the Jewish state in the Middle East can have an essential place alongside other transforming elements in this region which, as you admitted—and on this subject we certainly have the same opinion—is in need of profound changes on all levels in order for it to become what each of us wants it to be.

I emphasized before how delicate I felt both the process of harmonizing Israeli and Arab societies and then the process of integrating Israel into the Middle East would be. I also said that the positive factors I mentioned would not necessarily have much weight. Without this integration, the stability of the region will be precarious, but the necessary adaptations will come about of their own accord and we should not try to bring them on artificially or speed up the process.

JEAN LACOUTURE: Two questions. The first brings us back to what you have partially answered, but also has another aspect: Does Israel consider the dynamism of the Palestinians compatible with the idea of peace?

Then I want to ask, for the Sabras whom you have just described so well, does Zionism have the same force and meaning that it has for the people who were driven from Europe half a century ago by such terrible hardships? For those who are a product of the land, who were born there, isn't there something more static, more limited about this, and aren't they perhaps less drawn by the Messianic aspect of Zionism than those who were brought there through suffering, after having dreamed of Israel from afar for many years?

MAHMOUD HUSSEIN: May I expand your question a bit by adding something about the Sabras?

If their horizon is more limited as far as the Diaspora is concerned, is it a little wider, by contrast, where the Arabs are concerned?

SAUL FRIEDLÄNDER: I will have to disappoint you by answering only briefly and in a general way, for it is impossible to give a clear and definite answer to your questions.

Concerning the Sabras in relation to the Jewish world and their particular form of Zionism, two things, I think, can be said. Their Jewishness—if you can use that term—exists, there is no question

about it, whatever might be true about the weakening of religion in
Israel. The Sabras are perhaps less emotional about this in their
behavior than the people of the older generation; they do not
necessarily weep when they meet their brothers from New York or
Moscow, but I wouldn't say that there aren't tears in their eyes
when they see the immigrants arriving from the Soviet Union. It is
not simple. They are tied to Judaism by a whole tradition which is
passed on to them in their families and in school. In the end, they
are completely immersed in the atmosphere of a Jewish nation.

Their Zionism is perhaps different from that of the preceding
generations, it may be less rigid, but it exists. I think that except
for a small minority, which is not representative on a national
level, the youth in Israel would not say to you: "We do not want
immigrants." There are, however, causes for reticence on the part
of some. Here I open a large parenthesis: for the Sabras of Oriental
origin the immigration from Europe and the Soviet Union is a
problem. To them, the immigrants seem to be favored materially,
while they, young people born in the country, usually from the
poorest class, have not succeeded in acquiring what they consider
to be the strict minimum. Because of this there has been some
resentment expressed about the benefits given to the immigrants,
particularly the Russian Jews. But it seems to me that this is a
relatively temporary problem, which the government is trying to
correct as quickly as possible, realizing its potential danger.

Having closed the parenthesis, I will go on to say that in
Israel—and this includes the Sabras, particularly the Sabras—the
prevalent attitude remains basically Zionist—in the traditional
sense of the term—without being as emotional and as rigid as it
was among the Zionists of the past. The result—this should be
emphasized, and here I am repeating what I said before—is that we
can see a much greater sensitivity, understanding, respect, and
openmindedness concerning the other side of the Israeli reality, the
Arab side. In Israel the Jew from Russia continued to live in
Russia. I admire the old Russian pioneers for their character, their
strength and tenacity, but they understood neither the Arabs nor
their language. In spite of my respect for the very strong personality of Mrs. Golda Meir, I have always had the impression that for
her the Arab world was a mystery.

As for the attitude of the Sabras toward the outside world, it is marked by mistrust. This distrust of the Foreigner is a typical trait in the youth of any small country in the process of formation. On the whole, there is no doubt that the Sabra feels less obliged to pay careful attention to what the Foreigner says or does not say. Not that he will refuse foreign aid if it is necessary, but he does not have an obsession with "What will he say?" This attitude is perhaps expressed by a certain arrogance, but also by less docility, and by less submissiveness to powerful protectors.

MAHMOUD HUSSEIN: The picture you have just sketched of all the evidence of political and ideological renewal in Israel is very encouraging. The openness of heart and mind that you see in the Sabra youth is a real step toward the changes that I feel are essential for the future, if this openness is really expressed as an aspiration for the independence of the region from all foreign powers and as an aspiration to understand the hopes of the Arab people, in contrast to the superiority complex and "Western ethnocentricity" which has characterized Israeli ideology for so long.

While I don't want to be pessimistic, we should be realistic and say that the victory of this new spirit over the first generations of Zionists will not come about without upheaval and that the present Zionist establishment will not willingly give up the reins of power to people who want to shake their principal political tenets, nor will the American fund raisers for Israel welcome such a change. But we will let the future take care of this.

Finally, I would like to ask you one last question about the way in which you envisage the material and economic integration of Israel into the region.

SAUL FRIEDLÄNDER: Israel does not ask anything more than to integrate itself materially into the Middle East. In describing the phases of a political settlement and the necessity of withdrawal by stages, I also talked about a gradual normalization. I mentioned the free movement of people, the free circulation of goods, and finally, the fundamental aspect of this integration—joint efforts in certain areas in which the countries of the region could coordinate their efforts. As examples, one could think of nuclear centers, the desalination of sea water, the irrigation of certain desert areas. Egypt, for example, is going to regain the Sinai little by little, and will begin to want to develop it. Perhaps Egypt will do this alone, but since both Egypt and Israel will have nuclear centers, we don't see why these efforts, which will take many years, should not be integrated. For Israel the Negev, and for Egypt the Sinai—both of which are part of one desert—pose the same problem. Why must each work alone on either side of a barrier when the same sorts of work are required? This would clearly be an important mode of technological integration.

Nevertheless, the general economic problem remains complex. It is no great secret to you that Israeli economists are thinking about the economic aspects of the eventual peace: What do the national economies of the region have in common that can help lead to the political rapprochement between the two parties? The idea is simple; it is the same idea that Jean Monnet applied to Europe— economic integration can accelerate détente and help lead to political integration. Now the possible overlappings of the economies of Israel, the West Bank, and Jordan are clear; on the other hand, it is difficult to find the common aspects of the Israeli and Egyptian economies, except at the level of the large projects I mentioned. Each is orienting itself toward production of light equipment and consumer goods; in this plan, there would be more competition than cooperation.

Among Israel, the West Bank, and Jordan, the problem is simpler and, as you know, the process of economic integration has already begun. Israeli goods are sold on the West Bank and even farther away, in Jordan, perhaps even in Syria and Saudi Arabia, and vice versa. Considerable imports of various products also cross the Jordan from east to west. Common features such as these can be developed and coordinated to bring about an industrial specialization of the two parties.

In any case, this is not the essential thing...And perhaps it is unreal to talk about such long-term prospects when we don't know how things are going to develop in the immediate future, even tomorrow. And concerning tomorrow—I will end on this note— apart from all the calculations and all their nuances, what we need more than anything else, on both sides, is a great deal of imagination and not a little generosity.

MAHMOUD HUSSEIN: Throughout this dialogue we have tried to shed some light on all the aspects of the Arab-Israeli debate, which involves more than one hundred million people and which goes back to the beginning of the century. That is why we went back and looked at the past, paused at the present, and then looked forward to the future; that is why I have tried as far as possible to show the political diversity of the Arab world, at the governmental level as well as at the popular level.

A project of this kind carries with it numerous risks, particularly that of remaining on the surface of things, of schematizing or simplifying them, or of going into too much detail in some places and leaving allusions insufficiently explained in others. We have not been able to avoid any of these pitfalls. But the point of our project was to deal with everything and to do it together. You and I are not what is important in this book, it is our dialogue—this extended confrontation between Israeli thinking and Arab thinking, and the manner in which each unfolds and reacts to the other.

To what end? Not to arrive at formulas for diplomatic agreement between the present Arab and Israeli governments, nor to write two parallel and rival histories of the conflict. Rather, to feel our way and little by little try to find the conditions for a peace that could be accepted by the peoples, and not simply dictated by the governments. Friedländer does not see the rift between these two notions; I do. And that is why I have very clearly pointed to the difference between the period we are passing through at present—which for all Arabs is marked by the urgent need to realize the objectives of the October war—and the period that would follow if these objectives were essentially attained.

There is the possibility, now, of a formal agreement on Arab-Israeli coexistence, which would be based on withdrawal from the Arab territories occupied in 1967 and recognition of the Palestinian nation. But this agreement can lead to a period of renewed frustration, to dreams of future revenge, just as easily as it can lead to a period of deep change and common struggle for liberation.

A Common Ground for the Youth of Both Sides

JEAN LACOUTURE: In your opinion, what is this possibility based on?

MAHMOUD HUSSEIN: The present period of transition is marked by the unusual convergence of a certain number of interests, which are completely contradictory in the long run, but which for the time being are working together toward a common goal: the reshaping of the Middle East on a more rational basis than the one that followed the war of 1967—a reshaping which takes into account the change in the balance of forces that occurred after 1973. On this level we can say that to a certain degree there has been a meeting of minds among the United States, the Soviet Union, the governments of the Arab countries adjacent to Israel, and popular opinion within these countries.

Among all these parties there are obviously very significant differences, which stem from the limited interpretation given by the 22 November 1967 Security Council resolution to the demand for a sovereign Palestinian state, independent of both Israel and Jordan. But in the context of the joint effort by the superpowers to find a less precarious balance of forces than before, certain possible syntheses appear, which basically amount to the Arab interpretation of the November 22nd resolution, coupled with the recognition of the Palestinians' national status.

It is in Israel itself that we find the main resistance to this solution, within the powerful current represented by the Likud, the religious parties, and a wing of the Maarach that still seems to be quite influential. This coalition of forces, which has not made up its mind to recognize the basic demands of Arab dignity—demands which even the United States has had to integrate into its strategic calculations—will be capable for some time to come of blocking, endangering, even undermining the prospects that have opened up since October 1973. The citizens of Israel should know what this means—the loss of a unique psychological opportunity for the instinctive reconciliation of the peoples at a crucial moment when the Arabs, having regained confidence in themselves, are ready to recognize the Israelis as neighbors, but not as protectors.

Whether this opportunity is lost or not, now, really depends on those Israelis who are prepared to oppose the schemes of the Zionist old guard and who understand that it is essential for Israel to give back willingly and in good faith the rights that belong to the Arabs—instead of letting these rights be extracted with bad grace under pressure from the United States and through new confrontations. Why is this essential? Because the period of coexistence that will eventually be established will be very different depending on whether coexistence has been imposed on Israel, at the cost of immense human and material sacrifices, by a lengthy mobilization for war which the Arabs will have undertaken with a feeling of growing exasperation toward Israel—or whether coexistence climaxes a phase of fruitful transition, during which most of the Israelis have shown to the Arab world that they understand the principal aspirations of the Arabs, that they want the future to be based on the respect they feel for these aspirations, and that to this end they are prepared to put a halt to the actions of all the sentimentalists who dream of a great and conquering Israel.

The difference between these two approaches shows us the possible differences in the quality of coexistence. In the first case, the ability of the people to free their minds from Arab-Israeli antagonisms, in order to confront their internal problems, will remain limited. The mistrust, the animosity toward Israel will take even deeper root in each Arab; the feeling will persist that Israel is the age-old enemy, even if this enemy is momentarily immobilized by international agreements. Because of this, the revolutionary thrust of the Arab masses against the conservative Arab classes and new forms of international domination will be partially crippled, either by the fear of new Israeli aggressions, or by the call of all sorts of Arab demagogues for new preventive or offensive wars. . .

In the case of the second form of coexistence, on the other hand, there will be a great possibility for the Arab revolutionary movements, freed of the Israeli handicap, to move ahead wholeheartedly against the various conservative regimes or ward off American or Russian threats, and to turn naturally toward the most advanced currents in Israel, from whom they might expect not simply understanding, but a willingness to join them in a parallel struggle.

It was with the aim of helping to clear the ground for this second process that I entered into this dialogue with an Israeli, with Friedländer in particular, that is to say, an Israeli devoted to Zionism who does not envisage the long-term future as I do. Why him? Because right away he announced that it was necessary to give back to the Arabs their lost territories and to recognize the national status of the Palestinians—in terms that can be accepted by dozens, by hundreds of thousands of Israelis. And the future will depend on the capacity of these people, today, to tip the balance in favor of a minimal solution acceptable to the Arabs. As I have said before, this will not bring an end to all our problems— but it is certainly the precondition for all peaceful developments in the future.

I will not return to our differences over the possibility of Israel's integration into the Arab world by economic means. I have already said why I do not think this is possible. In my book on the Arabs today, I sketched out the priorities for peaceful development: the political and cultural adaptation of Israel to its Arab environment, without which all systems of Arab-Israeli economic exchange will lead, not to cooperation, but to competition, hostility, and war.

The key to these problems lies in a total break by Israel with the capitalist West, which has continued to be the prime obstacle to Arab independence.

That is why Friedländer's portrait of the new generation in Israel is so promising—and although this promise is still fragile, it is extremely precious in terms of the future. It is among these Sabras, who were born on the same soil as we were and who share our perspective on things, for whom the war in Europe is something in the past and who conceive of the future in an Arab milieu—it is among them that we may see the growth of a real understanding of Arab aspirations, particularly those of the Palestinians. It is among them that we may see the birth of a real willingness to break the ties with the West and find common ground with today's Arab youth.

Our young men and women, in fact, are not deceived by the false attractions of a massive return to the region by the United States. They are preparing to meet its challenge. They are aware of the new forms of Arab dependence that might appear in the future. The United States has finally acknowledged what the Soviet Union has known since 1956—the Arab peoples could not remain under foreign control for too long; their national dignity has become irrepressible. Washington has been forced to realize this, and that is why it has tempered its support of Israel by recognizing Arab national realities. Now it is banking on tying the Arab world to the periphery of its system of domination, through a flexible kind of economic integration which will play upon the psychological problems of the preceding period. And the Arab political generation which dominated the scene during that period, representing a rather weakly established bourgeoisie and a sentimental and verbose nationalism, has been incapable of resisting this new strategy. In fact, it is in the process of adopting it and becoming the advocate for it in the region.

The patriotic young people in the Arab countries have settled down to the enormous task of uncovering the mechanics of the new American threat and of mobilizing popular opinion against its principal agents—while staying on the alert for the dangers of Soviet infiltration under the cover of anti-American aid. At the same time, they must look for the concrete forms of solidarity between the various struggles for liberation among the Arab peoples, which are taking place at different levels of national and social maturity—some have already confronted the problems of peripheral capitalism in crisis, as in Egypt and Morocco, while others are still dealing with the elementary problems of national rebirth, as in Palestine.

In the Arab world these differences mean that there will be a complex succession of periods of anti-imperialist struggle, with many fronts, with changing priorities and various forms, which will go through high points and low points, moments of success and moments of failure, but which will all tend toward a more independent, more popular, and more united Arab world.

In this context, Israel will not be standing off to one side. It holds a place, a central place among us, beyond which its leaders have tried to block our view up to now. In the future some Israelis will be unable to conceive of any possible attitude other than that of continuing in the same direction as in the past. Everything will depend, then, on the concrete choices of the younger generation, the forces for peace in Israel. Will they let themselves be carried along in the old direction, or will they be able to find, in their own ways and through decisive struggles against those who remain nostalgic for the past, ways of joining with us to liberate our region?

JEAN LACOUTURE: Saul Friedländer, you have the floor now for your concluding remarks.

After a moment's hesitation, Saul Friedländer said that in the light of Mahmoud Hussein's last remarks he had nothing more to add...

To the moderator of the debate, this seemed to be the most fitting conclusion possible.

Paris, July-September 1974

Afterwords to the American Edition

Saul Friedländer

Jean Lacouture, the moderator of our debate, interpreted my last sentence to him as a step forward, as a sign that positions were being brought together at the end of the confrontation. As a matter of fact, the meaning of this sentence was different. When asked if I wished to add anything to Mahmoud Hussein's last statement, I answered that I had nothing to add, which meant that there was no point in repeating arguments that had been articulated many times during the debate. For me, this was a cautious expression of disappointment at our failure to establish a genuine dialogue and achieve real understanding. But was this disappointment entirely justified? Didn't the confrontation of our views, by the very fact that it took place, clarify issues and produce greater understanding of the opponent, even draw together some positions? Eight months have passed since this dialogue was recorded, and I believe the

This afterword is the translation of the text published with the Hebrew edition of the book. It was written in March 1975 and published in Israel at the end of April. Translated by the author.

time has come, with the publication of the Hebrew translation of
the book, to reexamine what was said in Paris, to reconsider its
significance, to stress once more some of the basic points.

Why, first of all, was it necessary to choose two dedicated
Marxists as Arab interlocutors and to create, thereby, further
difficulties in the discussion, beyond those already stemming from
the conflict as such? The first reason is that there are still very few
Arabs who are ready to engage in an open (and publishable)
discussion with an Israeli; Adel Rifaat and Bahgat Elnadi agreed to
such a discussion (and they explain their reasons in the book itself).
But, more important, my interlocutors are known as exponents of
the Palestinian position, and they were close to Palestinian circles.
As I believe—and I shall come back to it—that without a solution
of the Palestinian problem, no solution will be found to the
Israeli-Arab conflict, a dialogue with two Arabs who reflect the
perspective of many within the Palestinian national movement
seemed to me especially important. The Marxist arguments and
terminology are not alien to the Palestinian national movement and,
therefore, should not be seen as artificial obstacles.

The basic aim of this dialogue was to clarify fundamental
attitudes and contribute to a more realistic mutual perception
between opponents whose views have been distorted by the effects
of enduring conflict and the absence of any meaningful contact. For
me, it was also a way of understanding how pro-Palestinian Arabs
react to an extremely moderate, but firmly Zionist, Israeli position.
I hoped to find out whether political flexibility could satisfy the
basic Arab demands or whether the essence of the conflict is rooted
in an ideological confrontation that cannot be overcome. In addition, I wanted to convince prospective readers—especially Arab
readers—that a fundamentally Zionist position may be totally
unrelated to any aspirations toward territorial expansion, but that,
on the other hand, willingness to relinquish territories does not
imply any readiness to abandon the Zionist character of the State of
Israel. Finally, I felt a dialogue of this kind might allow us, the
Israelis, to clarify issues for ourselves. The political and ideological fog that has spread in our country and in the Diaspora since the
Six Day War, and thickened since the Yom Kippur War, blurs the

difference between what is essential and what is secondary. Many people now ask themselves where the line is that separates what is vital from what is only important.

The dialogue seems to indicate that, ultimately, Israeli political flexibility does not really satisfy the basic Arab aspiration: the disappearance of Zionism, that is, of a sovereign Zionist State of Israel, in order to create a democratic and multi-confessional State of Palestine. There is no reason why the reader should not be convinced that the Arab position, as alluded to in the dialogue, is not the real goal of the Arabs. In the discussion it was impossible to clarify this "aspiration" as such. My interlocutors insisted on the distinction between what is considered an ideal solution from their viewpoint, but a solution that will appear in an indeterminate future, and the concrete political aim; for them, the concrete political goal is the existence of two sovereign states on the territory of ex-mandatory Palestine. In the long run, history will do the rest...

It seems, in fact, that regarding this critical issue of the real aims of the Arabs and Palestinians, Rifaat and Elnadi had not yet succeeded in making up their minds. On the one hand, during the dialogue they took a line similar to that of the Palestine Liberation Organization's official stand, as expressed by Arafat at the United Nations. Later on, however, when interviewed on French radio, they declared their readiness, under certain conditions, to accept a Zionist State of Israel: "Zionist?" asked the astonished interviewer.—"Zionist," they confirmed. The absence of a clearly delineated policy is apparently not exceptional; it typifies the confusion on this issue within the entire Arab-Palestinian camp. The distinction between the immediate political aim and the long-term aspiration allows them, in principle, to establish a link between diametrically opposed attitudes, but this link, while pragmatic, is artificial and cannot hide a fundamental ambivalence.

It is difficult to foresee how the Palestinian-Arab position will crystallize on the basic issue of the long-range acceptance or rejection of a Zionist State of Israel, but one may suppose that our own initiatives will influence this decision. In any case, let us beware of slamming the door even one minute before it becomes absolutely clear that Israel has no other option.

The territorial-political "map" which I present in this dialogue is, in fact, an attempt to delineate, from my viewpoint, the minimum conditions required for peaceful coexistence between the Arabs and us, what we call "true peace." It is a map based on the stable and definitive relations between our neighbors and ourselves that should prevail after final resolution of the conflict. It should not be considered a territorial arrangement to be established in exchange for a formal treaty only, that is, without real peace conditions. My map is based on the assumption that real peace, if it can be achieved, is impossible if there are significant Israeli territorial annexations beyond the 1967 borders and no change in the present status of Jerusalem.

As has been made abundantly clear in the book, progress toward a definitive settlement can only be a symmetrical progression in stages. The entire process must be relatively slow, due to the very nature of the conflict and obstacles that stand in the path of normalization. It should be obvious that our discussion did not purport to deal with concrete political or strategic measures but rather with general principles. However, as far as the map is concerned, I tried to make the final aims clear and presented an outline of the path that could lead to them.

Many Israeli readers, I suppose, will reject the territorial arrangements proposed here, even if they are based on a definitive agreement, that is, "true peace." As far as I can see, we cannot be certain the Arabs will proceed toward true peace with Israel, even if they are promised restitution of the territories occupied in 1967, with very minor modifications. If they won't, there is nothing to discuss. But, if the Arabs express a willingness to strive for real peace, a readiness that must be manifested at each stage of the settlement process, then as far as I am concerned, true peace and the development of our state within relatively narrow borders, with the guaranteed right for Israeli citizens to travel to any spot in the whole territory of Palestine (as explained in the book), is preferable by far to keeping territories but perpetuating an endless conflict, with all that it implies.

One can also assume that many Israeli readers will strongly resist the concept of a Palestinian state in part of the territory of Palestine—and even the recognition of the centrality of the Palestinian problem in the conflict. My assumption, already stated, is that without solution of the Palestinian problem, there can be no end to the conflict. The antagonism between the Palestinians and us may possibly be unresolvable. Each act of terrorism strengthens our reluctance to talk. In any case, semi-solutions to this problem are no longer possible (there may have been the possibility of a Jordano-Palestinian solution between the Six Day War and the Rabat Conference, but it no longer seems realistic).

One major point bears emphasis: only if the Palestinians recognize a sovereign State of Israel and declare their readiness to establish peaceful and stable relations with that state can successful negotiations become possible. A more subtle point (which may not be obvious in our country): my attitude toward the Palestinians is not based on political arguments alone; it also derives from a particular conception of the need for the self-limitation of Zionism. For me, the lines written by Ahad Haam in 1920 are still relevant: "This historical right [of the Jewish people to establish itself in Palestine—S.F.] does not cancel the right of the other inhabitants of the country, who come in the name of the concrete right bestowed by the very fact of their living and working here for generations. For them, too, this land is their national home in the present, and they, too, have the right to develop their national potential according to their ability. This situation, therefore, turns Palestine into a land which belongs in common to different peoples, in which each tries to build his national home. . ." If we replace the term "national home" with "state," we arrive at a position identical to the one I have tried to express in the dialogue.

Some among us oppose the idea of a Palestinian state because of attachment to all of the land of Israel; others are aware of the security risks involved, and, clearly, the acts of sabotage reinforce this awareness. Sometimes both attitudes are combined. However, it seems that even among those who are not in favor of annexing the West Bank and Gaza Strip, and among those who know that the security problems may eventually be resolved, there is profound resistance to granting sovereign rights to the Palestinians in part of Palestine. I believe this resistance derives partly from the latent fear that recognition of the rights of the Palestinians means, in itself, some measure of recognition of the justice of their arguments against us, and may, therefore, eventually imply a questioning of the very basis of Zionism.

Those who read the arguments of my interlocutors on the Palestinian question, or those who know these arguments from other sources, may recognize that the essential difference between these arguments and the Zionist perspective lies in the fact that the theses of the Palestinians can be generalized and applied to other situations, in other places and periods, whereas the basis of our position is the very uniqueness of our situation and of our ties with the land of Israel. We are, therefore, faced with two entirely different levels of reality and of argumentation. This is the basic difficulty inherent in the search for an understanding between the Palestinians and ourselves, but this also immunizes each side against the arguments of the other. This being said, we, the Israelis, should find it easier to understand the general arguments of the Palestinians than they, the Palestinians, to understand the unique Jewish-Israeli position. Hence, it seems logical for us to acknowledge that there is some justice in the Palestinian position, even before they can recognize the justice in ours. This would not be a sign of weakness or self-doubt. On the contrary, it would be an expression of our ability to assess reality and preserve fundamental intellectual and moral values. After all, if we do not make every possible effort to preserve both our sense of reality and our sense of justice, shall we not be weakening the position of Zionism, nurtured from the effort to find a just and realistic solution to the Jewish problem?

* * * * *

During the dialogue my interlocutors stressed the importance of social and economic forces and interests for the understanding of the Arab-Israeli conflict. I opposed this Marxist frame of reference because of its simplistic character and its obvious inadequacy to explain this conflict: the major elements of the Israeli-Arab confrontation are to be found, in my view, in the realm of collective reminiscences and aspirations, in collective myths and emotions. At the beginning of the dialogue I mentioned the explosion of collective hatred against Israel that shook the Arab world on the eve of the Six Day War. Now we are facing a kind of polarization:

on the one hand, we can notice growing signs of moderation among some Arabs but, on the other, positions of extreme hatred are intensifying and solidifying within an important "rejection front." No one can tell which of these two currents will prevail, and this is, in the end, the fundamental uncertainty that gnaws at our hope for a settlement. Even within the limited context of this dialogue, this uncertainty casts its shadow on its positive elements.

Mahmoud Hussein

In deciding to initiate the "dialogue" with Saul Friedländer, we were drawing practical conclusions from analysis of the changes in the Middle East brought about by the October war. We were not prompted by a sudden burst of idealism, which might have led us to make an abstraction of the enormous gap that lay between us. If this had been the case, our idealism would have quickly vanished with the first terrorist action of the Palestinians in Galilee, or the first raid by the Israelis in southern Lebanon.

We do not hide the fact that we had no thought of dialogue before the Ramadan War. To talk with a Zionist while his country was pretending to act as arbitrator of the region's destiny, while his government was transforming the occupied status of the Arab territories through annexation, while the Israeli army was intervening with impunity wherever it wished, would have been a kind of psychological capitulation. We felt that the Arabs had long years of humiliation ahead of them before this situation could be changed: having crippled the Palestinian resistance, the regimes in control

Translated from the French by Paul Auster and Lydia Davis.

seemed resigned to their own impotence, and there were no revolutionary forces among the Arabs capable of radically changing this course of things. Except for a few hundred young revolutionaries, there was no one in Israel challenging government policy, and the Meir-Dayan-Galili trio reigned undisturbed. It seemed to us that the future would be blocked for a long time to come.

Under these conditions, dialogue was not only unthinkable, but useless; a dialogue has no meaning unless it takes place in the context of an objective process of rapprochement between the two parties, unless it adds a certain dynamism to an already solid hope for change. This hope did not exist. Arab preoccupations were therefore concentrated on a single point: reversing the situation in such a way as to give us back our dignity and self-confidence.

It was the October war that brought this about.

The results were not exactly what we had hoped for—an outburst of popular forces that would have turned the war into a revolutionary struggle for liberation and led the way to fraternal resolution of the conflict that has set Jews and Arabs against one another for half a century. What we had hoped for was that the two peoples would begin to recognize and accept one another. But the 1973 war, which was led by narrow social interests, could do no more than initiate arduous deals over borders and international guarantees.

But the confrontation, nevertheless, had some positive results; at the same time that it rekindled Arab pride, it proved to the Israelis that their security could not be based indefinitely on the gamble of military superiority. No people in the world has ever been able to survive among hostile neighbors by the force of arms alone; sooner or later, if the factors of hostility do not diminish, the coalition of the weaker parties gives birth to an efficient force of retaliation and the solitary party is little by little undermined by the illusion of its own invulnerability. This is a law of history, which has been confirmed countless numbers of times over the centuries, and Israel is no exception to it.

Two emotional worlds, two states of mind, which until then had been completely separate—Israeli arrogance and Arab bitterness—received a great shock in October 1973, and from this event, which destroyed the previous balance of forces (without, however, establishing a new equilibrium), a fragile hope was born—that each camp would be willing to listen to the other, respect the other's suffering, and finally, after a state of permanent war, attempt to live together in a state of coexistence.

The conditions for realizing this hope could not be defined arbitrarily; they were the product of the fundamental and irrepressible aspirations of the peoples of the region. If Israel wanted to affirm its right to exist, the Arabs wanted to affirm their right to sovereignty—which implied the withdrawal from the territories occupied in June 1967 and the recognition of a sovereign State of Palestine in its historic homeland. If Israel counted on being admitted into the Middle East by its neighbors, the Arabs counted on being assured that Israel would stop acting against them as a base of aggression and expansion.

The dialogue between us and a Zionist Israeli not only became possible, at that point, but also seemed practical. It allowed us to measure the distance that separated the two camps and estimate our chances for beginning the process of coexistence—that is, of creating that area, particularly difficult to reach, in which our mutual distrust would temporarily disappear, giving way to a sort of psychological no man's land, a double negation of hatred, where the possibility of mutual acceptance could enter, little by little.

Somewhere, that area existed—which was the source of our optimism. But this optimism could only be cautious, reserved, and conditional; for we knew—and the eight months that have passed since our dialogue was recorded have all too sadly confirmed this—that there was also an enormous obstacle blocking our way in the search for common ground. This obstacle is the ideology of the Israeli leaders today, the majority of whom still see the Arabs in the same way that the Zionist colonialist of the early part of the century saw them—as a people without a past, without a culture, without aspirations—and, in a word, without any real historical weight. Between Ben-Gurion, who said as early as 1917 that Palestine was empty "both historically and morally," and Rabin, who stated in February 1975 on French television that Israel was "the bastion of civilization confronting the Arab Middle Ages"— nothing has changed!

If the majority of the Israeli leaders still prefer to hold on to the Arab territories rather than put an end to the state of belligerency, if they continue to link the security of Israel with military superiority rather than with mutual acceptance by Arabs and Israelis, it is because they do not believe that the Arabs are their equals, because they mistrust the Arab world and can conceive of no peace other than one imposed by force.

This is the main obstacle that stands—and has always stood—between the peoples of the region. This is the obstacle that must be removed before a real change of heart can take place.

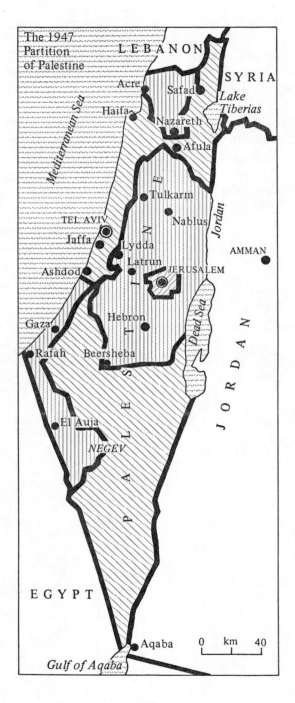

The 1947
Partition
of Palestine

LEBANON

SYRIA

Acre

Safad

Lake
Tiberias

Mediterranean Sea

Haifa

Nazareth

Afula

Tulkarm

Jordan

TEL AVIV

Nablus

AMMAN

Jaffa

Lydda

Latrun

JERUSALEM

Ashdod

Dead Sea

Hebron

JORDAN

Gaza

Rafah

Beersheba

P A L E S T I N E

El Auja

NEGEV

EGYPT

Aqaba

0   km   40

Gulf of Aqaba

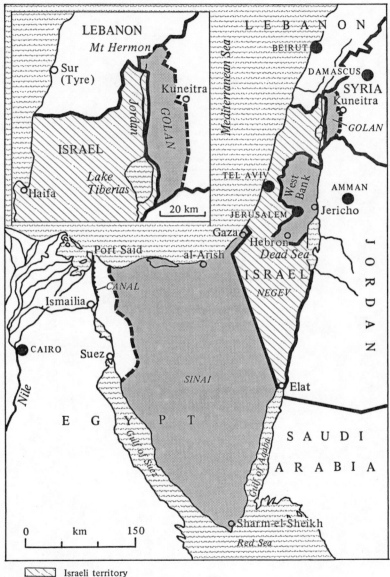

Israeli territory

Territory occupied by Israel since June 1967

Cease-fire lines between Israel and Egypt (Jan. 1974) and Syria (May 1974)

223

DATE DUE

MR 2 6 '79			
AP 9 '79			
AP 23 '79			
MR 2 7 '81			
AP 2 2 '81			
FE 21 '86			
MAR 7 '86			
APR 1 3 '87			
GAYLORD			PRINTED IN U.S.A